Advance praise for *The Ascent of a Leader*

"Leadership is all about relationships. This book is a must-read for those who want to lead in relationship building."
—C. William Pollard, chairman, The ServiceMaster Company

"*The Ascent of a Leader* powerfully cuts through all areas of life. I am confident these principles will profoundly enrich the leader's marriage, family, social, and corporate relationships."
—Mike Singletary, NFL Hall of Fame

"The leadership journey that *The Ascent of a Leader* describes so well is truly an extraordinary experience, although not for the faint of heart. If we stay with the journey as the authors advise though, it takes us beyond our own minds and imaginations and leaves us astounded by grace. I would recommend this book for any leaders who are sincerely attracted to the challenge of letting God take them to places they've never been before."
—Janet Hagberg, director, Silent Witness National Initiative; author, *Real Power* and *The Critical Journey*

"This powerful and inspiring book points to vital steps that can help readers move from selfishness to selflessness, from self-sufficiency to God-sufficiency. True leaders are spawned, the authors write, by small groups of faithful people in which participants can be healed and restored, and broken loose from human bondage to do the real work of the world."
—George Gallup Jr., chairman, Gallup International Institute

"*The Ascent of a Leader* represents a ground-breaking blend of the technical and character aspects of leadership."
—Bill Hybels, chairman, The Willow Creek Association

"This inspiring book is essential reading for those who seek to earn the respect of the emerging generation who hunger for leaders whose personal and professional lives are centered on character and dignity."
—Dick Capen, former U.S. ambassador to Spain, chairman and publisher of *The Miami Herald*

"Climbing the ladder of success is a driving passion for many in today's corporate America, but too often character is compromised on the way up. *The Ascent of a Leader* helped me think through both motives and means to true success."
—John Beckett, president, R. W. Beckett Corporation; author, *Loving Monday: Succeeding in Business Without Selling Your Soul*

"Fresh, introspective, noble—this book contrasts the conventional leadership climb to sacred truth, mature living, and selfless achievement. The authors deftly describe what it means to lead by example and answer one of life's great questions, 'Why do people follow?'"
—William Boyajian, president, Gemological Institute of America

"No matter what your leadership style, *The Ascent of a Leader* will make you reassess it. I hope that future leaders will adopt the important creative suggestions and insights in this book. A must-read for us all."
—Wallace R. Hawley, founder, InterWest Partners; vice chairman, Center for Economic Policy Research, Stanford University

"A fascinating journey about personal relationships and the importance of character, integrity, and faith, which prepares one to step up the ladder in leadership."
—Jerry Colangelo, president and chief executive officer, Phoenix Suns; managing general partner, Arizona Diamondbacks

"This outstanding book of principles provides leaders with unusual how-to's and practical steps for developing character. *The Ascent of a Leader* is a remarkable look at how young leaders learn to serve others and how older leaders learn to reach their destiny."
—Matthew Parker, president, Institute for Black Family Development

"Today we see so many visible and disappointing examples of fallen and falling leaders . . . in business, in government, in sports, even in religion. *The Ascent of a Leader* provides important insights into the critical importance of character development (rather than just skill development) in helping you fulfill your potential as a positive leader."
—Dale Gifford, chief executive officer, Hewitt Associates

"A must-read for those wanting to make a difference in their businesses, communities, and families. A perfect blend of wisdom, compassion, and practical experience!"
—Jay Abraham, director of sports, Franklin Covey

"This book is a profound and unique answer to the questions of our tumultuous society . . . uncompromising character development produces profound influence and leadership ability."
—Naomi Rhode, past president, National Speakers Association and '97 Cavett Winner

"This profound and timely book teaches us how to live well and to lead wisely. *The Ascent of a Leader* creatively shows us how to center our lives in unchanging principles that produce an enduring influence in all our relationships."
—John R. Castle Jr., executive vice president (retired), EDS

"No topic is more timely for our culture than to learn how character and influence develop in relationships over a lifetime. *The Ascent of a Leader* shows us how to lay hold of it."
—Larry Crabb, best-selling author, psychologist, distinguished scholar in residence

"Due to the current lack of spiritual leadership in our country, the message in these pages is deeply needed at this time across our land. It clearly promotes a principle-based pathway of leadership that fosters hope, trust, reconciliation, and character."
—John M. Perkins, founder, John M. Perkins Foundation for Reconciliation and Development

"*The Ascent of a Leader* is truly a 'holy' book for anyone on the leadership path. As a young leader of a family business, this book provided a roadmap (or ladder!) for me on how to lead from values and integrity."
—Louise Slater, chairman of the board Consolidated Systems, Inc.

"Having spent several years on the staff at West Point contemplating the development of leaders of character, I find in *The Ascent of a Leader* a powerfully insightful, honest, and encouraging model for practice by leaders who genuinely seek to grow in character and in the impact for good that such leadership makes possible."
—Larry Donnithorne, author, *The West Point Way of Leadership: From Fostering Principled Leadership to Practicing It*

"Successful leadership is a spiritual journey. In these inspiring pages, you will find a rare map for your soul, a map that can help you negotiate the thrills, risks, and lonely moments we all visit as leaders. You may also discover a yearning to share this map and journey with emerging leaders of the next generation."
—Karen Brugler, manager, Health Care Consulting Practice, Ernst & Young, LLP

"This book, written from the experiences of three gifted leaders, gives practical suggestions of how one can climb the character ladder, the ladder of self-discovery, each of which draws one to his or her true self."
—Tom Phillips, president, International Students, Inc.

"We live at a time in history when there is a pronounced vacuum in leadership. Our need is for clear, inspiring, and above all timeless teaching on the subject of leadership. *The Ascent of a Leader* powerfully provides us with all these and more."
—Michael Card, best-selling composer, author, teacher

"As each chapter unfolded, I found myself desiring the next. If you want to be prepared for a meaningful leadership opportunity when it arrives, then this book is for you."
—Karsten Louis Solheim, executive vice president, Karsten Manufacturing Corporation

"A fresh—revolutionary—look at leadership. This book will not just change your leadership style, it will change you and the lives you touch."
—Daniel Dominguez, CPA/partner, BDO Seidman, LLP

"*The Ascent of a Leader* addresses the two most important questions leaders—actually anyone—must answer if their lives and work are to have meaning: Who are you? And who cares? Character shapes cultures and culture nourishes character. Who you are makes a difference."
—Walter C. Wright Jr., president, Regent College

"My job of training young managers for The Weather Channel during its startup would have been much easier if this resource had been available. It will also spark a renaissance for senior managers who may have forgotten how or why they climbed the ladder."
—Hugh Eaton, startup business manager, The Weather Channel

"*The Ascent of a Leader* shows how character is a lifelong building process between God and yourself that then translates into leadership."
—Karl Eller, chairman, Eller Media Company

"Superb, a must-read for everyone who would lead others with God's help by developing extraordinary character."
—Robert A. Fulton, chairman and chief executive officer, Web Industries, Inc.

"In this remarkable and helpful book, the authors carefully and clearly help us to understand that leaders are made, not necessarily born. Anyone who aspires to leadership—young or old, male or female—will be helped immensely by this significant publication."
—Ted W. Engstrom, president emeritus, World Vision

About Leadership Catalyst

The mission of Leadership Catalyst is to produce a generation of leaders who can be trusted. This is accomplished through a four-stage learning process:

Owning influence
Leading from strengths
Protecting weaknesses
Transferring truth

Team-based and mentor-driven in its design, this learning process develops a leader's influence, producing a convergence of calling, character, competency, and community. Delivery of the learning process is implemented through fellows of the Catalyst Institute.

Established in 1995, Leadership Catalyst is recognized as an international resource for helping leaders learn how to develop authentic environments of trust, character, vision and productivity.

For additional information on Leadership Catalyst, please contact us directly:

Leadership Catalyst, Inc.
5060 N. 19th Ave. Suite 317
Phoenix, AZ 85015
602-249-7000 (Phoenix area)
888-249-0700 (Toll-free)
602-249-0611 (Fax)
e-mail: info@leadershipcatalyst.org
Website: www.leadershipcatalyst.org

The Ascent of a Leader

How Ordinary Relationships Develop
Extraordinary Character and Influence

Bill Thrall

Bruce McNicol

Ken McElrath

Foreword by Ken Blanchard

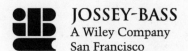

JOSSEY-BASS
A Wiley Company
San Francisco

Jossey-Bass books and products are available through most bookstores. To contact Jossey-Bass directly, call (888) 378-2537, fax to (800) 605-2665, or visit our website at www.josseybass.com.

Substantial discounts on bulk quantities of Jossey-Bass books are available to corporations, professional associations, and other organizations. For details and discount information, contact the special sales department at Jossey-Bass.

 Manufactured in the United States of America on Lyons Falls Turin Book. This paper is acid-free and 100 percent totally chlorine-free.

Library of Congress Cataloging-in-Publication Data

Thrall, Bill.
 The ascent of a leader : how ordinary relationships develop extraordinary character and influence / Bill Thrall, Bruce McNicol, and Ken McElrath. — 1st ed.
  p. cm.
 Includes bibliographical references and index.
 ISBN 0-7879-4766-0 (alk. paper)
  1. Leadership—Religious aspects. 2. Character. 3. Success—Religious aspects.
 4. Self-realization. I. McNicol, Bruce. II. McElrath, Ken. III. Title.
 BL626.38 .T48 1999
 291.6'1—dc21   99-6328

FIRST EDITION
HB Printing   10 9 8 7 6 5 4 3

Contents

List of Figures

To our wives,
Grace Thrall, Janet McNicol, and Donna McElrath,
who in sharing our hardships, our joys, our burdens, and our
blessings, gave us the encouragement we needed to press on.

Foreword

A lot of people think our nation is in a crisis. The general public keeps talking about how fed up they are with the government's way of running the show in Washington, D.C. Though I tend to be a little more optimistic about our nation's future, the truth remains that we face great challenge in this era of constant change.

Today's leaders seem to have competence and charisma, but they fall short in the character dimension. Anytime we have people voting along party lines on important values issues, you know we are in trouble. Over the past several decades, character has been an assumed part of a leader's makeup. This assumption has led to questionable personal and corporate results in the worlds of business, government, education, and the social sector at large. We can no longer assume that good character comes with leadership. Although I think a crisis looms on the horizon, we still have an opportunity to get back to the basics and overcome our present problems.

That's why I'm so excited about *The Ascent of a Leader*. In this book, Bill Thrall, Bruce McNicol, and Ken McElrath examine the process of developing character in our leaders, our relationships, our community, and, most important, in ourselves. Though molding your character can often be a painful process, this book shows us the priceless rewards of developing ordinary relationships into extraordinary character over a lifetime.

The journey to developing character naturally leads to personal significance and often helps you see what your life purpose is. By committing to this process, you will begin to understand what true leadership is all about: authentically influencing your community through a life of significance.

In my many years of management training, I have discovered that you can talk about having values until you're blue in the face. But when there are gaps between what you say and how you behave, then you need to take a long look in the mirror. Leaders of character must give more than lip service to their values. Character is formed by acting on what you know to be true in your heart, not just by what comes out of your mouth.

I recommend, Bill, Bruce, and Ken's book because it shows principles of leadership that can be applied by anyone in a position of influence. *The Ascent of a Leader* challenges us to take a look at our own priorities—where we are today—and equips us with ways to move forward in the process of developing ourselves and others.

Enjoy your ascent to a more meaningful life. Always keep in mind that, even though character is often tested in isolation, it is developed through your interactions with the people who count on you.

Ken Blanchard
Coauthor of *The One-Minute Manager*

Preface

The Ascent of a Leader articulates some very practical ideas for developing extraordinary character and influence in ordinary relationships. But do not be fooled by the words *practical* or *ordinary*. We do not mean to imply a simplistic methodology or a shallow technique for ascending to new heights of power. Rather, we say "practical" because these principles can be *practiced*. Indeed, they *must* be practiced to be understood in the fullest sense rather than just understood intellectually. When we say "ordinary" relationships we do not mean "common" in the negative sense of the word but in the positive sense. We mean that those around you right now, in your family, workplace, or church setting, can participate in an uncommon process that produces extraordinary results, one of which is becoming the kind of leader that others want to follow.

One of the best and worst things about writing is that you must eat your own words. To write with authenticity, you must not only think good thoughts but also chew on them, swallow them, digest them, and test their potency. Perhaps some can write in a detached way, simply typing words and shuffling them about into more pleasing patterns, but we have not had such easy going. In writing about ordinary relationships, our own relationships have been extraordinarily tested. In defining and exploring the foundations of influence, the foundations of our own influence have been rattled and redefined. Our abilities to consistently live the principles of this book have been stretched to the limits. We do not, therefore, take any of the statements we have made lightly. You will find no utopian vision here.

The principles are for everyday people in everyday situations. They are not idealistic. They are not for the select few. They are not restricted in their application. They are intended to be put into practice by women and men from all walks of life, in any relational context. But there's a catch. In practicing them, you will find how simply revolutionary such principles can be. They cannot be toyed with like the latest diet fad, visited for a couple of weeks and then cast off with a "been there, done that." They require a dramatic rethinking of how you live your life and why you live with others. Still, they retain their simplicity, despite their profundity. Even children can understand and apply these principles with success.

Perhaps our children even understand them better. A carpenter named Jesus knew this. He once huddled a bunch of children around him and said, "Whoever becomes simple and elemental again, like this child, will rank high in God's kingdom," and "Unless you accept God's kingdom in the simplicity of a child, you'll never get in."[1] Children understand the simple things. The important things. The profound things. They don't bother taking the time to pick truth or love apart until either becomes powerless to do them any good. They simply trust truth and love with their hearts, because they trust the relationship between the gift and the giver. Jesus loved them. This they knew. Not because the Bible told them so but because Jesus did. And he demonstrated it to them each day. So when he called, they came running with reckless abandon.

We do not wish to encourage childish recklessness, but we do encourage a type of childlike abandon as you read. Most children can switch gears rather quickly when something better comes along—leaving a toy behind to grasp the playful, inviting hand of a parent, for instance. Adults have a harder time embracing change, especially when it comes to letting go of patterns that have taken years to develop. But truth can invade our patterns, if we let it, inviting us to childlike abandon. Truth acts as a mirror. It can show us where we have been, and it can tell us something about ourselves. Truth invites us to change for the better.

Look for the truths contained in this book and ask yourself some questions. Will practicing these principles lead me to love or to indifference? And for which do I want to be known? Will applying these ideas inspire vision and hope or complacency and apathy? And to which do I want to lead others? Perhaps most important, abandon yourself to those truths that help you see who you really are and become who you want to become.

Acknowledgments

We owe a great debt to many in our own lives who have helped us flesh out the principles in this book. These people have spoken truth to us when we needed to hear it. They have loved us despite our own failures and frailties. In short, they have helped us become something far better than we could have become on our own.

Thanks to the board, staff, and advisory council of Leadership Catalyst, Inc., for their timeless encouragement. Special thanks go to Ellen Antill, Wendy Hancock, Mark Carver, Mike Hamel, David Sanford, and Vesta Walker, whose practical care, expertise, and affirmation have inspired us to do more than we thought we could do. Thanks to the women and men of Open Door Fellowship for living these truths, to Leadership Network for championing this book before it was birthed, and to the board and staff of Interest Associates and other related organizations who helped us gain many of these insights. The people of Jossey-Bass deserve rich praise for their publishing expertise and encouragement, as do the volunteer readers and researchers who contributed their insights to enrich this message. Finally, we would like to thank the many individuals who have given us permission to use their stories, and U.S. Senator Jon Kyl in particular for his many helpful story suggestions.

If you would like to know more about Leadership Catalyst, Inc., and its programs, please contact us at (888) 249-0700, or visit our website, http://www.leadershipcatalyst.org.

Phoenix, Arizona
July 1999

Bill Thrall
Bruce McNicol
Ken McElrath

Introduction

The Ascent of a Leader is about rising above what you can accomplish or become on your own. Whereas many leaders have been trained in how to reach their personal best, this book invites you to a place where talents, titles, politics, and diplomas alone cannot take you.

To rise above and beyond your individual best, you need a certain kind of environment in which to live and work. Such an environment would nurture the integration of heart and hand, word and deed, spirituality and everyday life. It would nourish your relationship with God and kindle your connections with those around you. This environment and the relationships it spawns would help you become more than a leader. They would help you become the kind of leader whom others want to follow.

This kind of leadership is possible because this kind of environment is possible. Indeed, it even exists today in a variety of communities and contexts. This book will help you cultivate such a climate. Wherever this environment infiltrates a culture, a sense of safety and protection pervades. Productivity and creativity blossom. Trust flourishes. And of great significance to leaders and followers everywhere, character matures.

Why is character important?

Character—the inner world of motives and values that shapes our actions—is the ultimate determiner of the nature of our leadership. It empowers our capacities while keeping them in check. It distinguishes those who steward power well from those who abuse power. Character weaves such values as integrity, honesty, and selfless service into the fabric of our lives, organizations, and cultures.

In the past, some assumed that the family would own the task of developing character. But many of our families seem to have forgotten how. Others thought the church would shoulder this role. But according to separate studies by both Gallup and Purdue University, religion is declining among leaders.[1] Although the number of churchgoing folk has held steady over the past seventy years, during the past ten years the significance of faith in the workplace has steadily declined. This trend is unfortunate, especially when we realize the positive impact religious faith can have on leadership.

Consider a study by Frank Toney, a professor and the director of the Executive Initiative Institute, and Merrill Oster, a CEO and former *Inc.* Magazine Entrepreneur of the Year. According to their research, those who consciously apply religious teachings during their daily activities attain their goals more consistently, rank higher in virtually all leadership measurement instruments, and achieve greater satisfaction, net worth, and personal fulfillment.[2] Not bad.

But of course the question remains, What teachings? How do we make religious faith practical in the day-to-day world we live in, particularly in positions of influence? Is there a process for developing the inner values that direct actions and performance? Can parents learn it? Can CEOs learn it? How about church and nonprofit leaders? And if they can, how can such a process be implemented? And what does God have do to with it?

We believe there is a God who is intimately aware of and involved in our lives. And God cares about such important questions. We have written this book primarily to the nine people out of ten who believe in the existence of God and who frequent some place of worship.[3] Each of the coauthors claims a distinctly Christian faith, rooted in a biblical understanding of grace and truth. But we make no overt attempt in this book to convert you to our faith. Instead we set forth an intentional process and the principles we have learned as straightforwardly and simply as we know how, in the hopes that they can be broadly applied in a variety of areas.

Overview of the Contents

Chapter One explores the relationship between our inner lives and our influence. Why do we need to face the deeper issues of life and leadership? Why would we want to?

Chapter Two describes a profound dilemma of today's leaders while exposing the roots of the crisis. What dilemma? The ladder to success most of us know does not necessarily lead to positive influence, deeper relationships, or an enduring legacy.

Chapters Three and Four establish the essential framework for the climb up what we call the *character ladder*. In addition to rungs, all ladders need rails, the vertical posts that hold the rungs in place. One rail of the character ladder is environment, the subject of Chapter Three. The other rail is relationships, the subject of Chapter Four. In these chapters, you will find how critical both are to sustaining and nurturing character and influence during your ascent.

Chapters Five, Six, and Seven challenge the status quo by redefining success to include the first three rungs of the character ladder. The chapters prescribe intentional choices that, when carried out in the context of ordinary relationships, can help you avoid many common leadership drains and dysfunctions.

Chapter Eight introduces the pitfalls and promise of continuing your ascent, which can appear rather frightening at the character ladder's critical fourth rung. Chapter Nine follows closely by describing the particular kind of testing the fourth rung requires. You will learn how to avoid falling or slipping away from your destiny and how to lead with greater objectivity as you step to the fifth and final rung.

Chapter Ten describes the fifth rung—discovering your destiny—and demonstrates the unique nature of a leader's influence from this height, as compared to leadership from the shorter ladder of capacity development. Then, in Chapter Eleven, we encourage you to prepare for seven challenges a fifth-rung leader must face.

The book closes with some practical parting advice and personal examples of implementing the principles found in the previous chapters. It also offers a challenge to apply in meaningful ways what you have learned.

A Universal Challenge

As you explore the principles in these pages, we encourage you to consider carefully the issues and questions raised in each chapter. We realize we have only cast a pebble into a vast lake, but we hope the ripples will gain amplitude through your careful study. Our hope hinges on your willingness to stop and consider the implications of what we have said.

The stories told in this book come from a variety of sources: personal experience, friends, biographies, and storybooks. The personal stories are true. We use our own first names when the stories come from our own lives. In an effort to protect the privacy of individuals, we have changed such identifying characteristics as name, location, and—in some instances—gender and occupation. In other cases you'll learn some little-known facts about well-known people—things about their lives that produced extraordinary character and influence.

This is not a book about management, although the principles it contains may dramatically affect how you manage. It is not a book about methodology, although the truths it espouses may profoundly affect your methods. *The Ascent of a Leader* is not about guaranteeing that your kids will turn out OK, avoiding marital difficulties, building a better church, or increasing the bottom line, although it speaks to each in a variety of ways.

Instead, this book is about becoming the kind of leader whom others want to follow. It's about finding God's plan for your life and following it, and about leading others where they need to go. Whether you are a seasoned leader or just starting out in your career, a leadership expert or someone just beginning to understand leadership issues, we hope you will consider this book to be an invitation to climb higher.

The Ascent of a Leader is written for mothers. It's written for husbands. It's written for bosses, secretaries, pastors, teachers, students, artists, and factory workers. It's written for the leader in all of us—for ordinary people who want to develop extraordinary character. But it is written by fellow climbers. We invite you to explore these principles, relationships, and environments with us, not in theory alone but also in practice. Together, with God's help, we truly can make a difference in the twenty-first century—in our families, our communities, our companies, our government, and even our world.

Chapter One

A Different Ladder to Success

If you are to step out into the unknown, the place
to begin is with the exploration of the inner
territory.

—*James Kouzes and Barry Posner*

"Close the emergency doors!"

"They're already closed, Sir," the first officer replied to the captain, whom he would have addressed as E. J. under less stressful conditions.

"Send to the carpenter and tell him to sound the ship," responded the captain. But the carpenter had already perished in the attempt to make repairs. As the hull rapidly took on water, the instruments on the bridge clearly indicated the ship's rapidly declining chances of survival.

While the steam sirens screamed in agony, the captain barked out several orders at once: "Wire distress signals," "Fire the rockets in case any ship can offer assistance," "All hands on deck." One wonders what other thoughts and emotions stirred in his heart just then.

Less than one year earlier, the aging captain had tarnished his excellent record in an embarrassing collision with the HMS *Hawke*. Soon thereafter, he had damaged his newly repaired ship again by sailing it over a submerged wreck. After patching up the broken propeller blade, the captain had determined to patch up his reputation to quell rumors of his deteriorating capacities. This voyage was to have done just that.

Sticking his head into the radio room, the captain directed, "Send the call for assistance."

"What call shall I send?" the Marconi operator asked.

"The regulation international call for help. Just that," came E. J.'s reply as he hurried away.

When the captain began this journey, he set a course. He set the speed. He alone was responsible for the safety of the ship and its passengers. But the course he set took his ship into peril, even though he had been warned of the danger. And the speed he set ultimately determined their fate.

Although policy clearly dictated "moderate speed and maximum comfort," the captain had treated his new charge like a sports car on a road with no speed limits. He had thought that arriving ahead of schedule would be just the trick to remove the stain from his reputation.

During the most dangerous part of the journey, the confident captain had left his third-in-command on the bridge while he boasted to his dinner guests how the ship could be cut into three sections and each would float. He believed the ship to be unsinkable.

Little more than an hour after this boast, he issued his last command: "You have done your duty boys; now every man for himself."[1]

Captain Edward J. Smith perished with more than one thousand other passengers in the icy Atlantic that night. His reputation went down with the *Titanic*.

Deeper Issues

Each of us leaves a legacy. Every organization makes its mark. Most of us strive to avoid such a disastrous end. And perhaps we can even identify the dangers, as could Captain Smith. When a friend asked earlier what could possibly bring such a ship down, Smith had replied, "The big icebergs that drift into warmer water. . . . If a vessel should run on one of these reefs half her bottom might be torn away. Some of us would go to the bottom with the ship."[2]

Often it's what we don't see on the surface that can bring us down: the deeper issues of life that affect who we are and all we do. Like Captain Smith, we may become forgetful of those deeper issues and dangers when we set out to accomplish a goal or achieve a better reputation—at least until those issues stare us in the face—but by then, it may be too late to avoid the consequences.

Many leaders never come face-to-face with an iceberg. Instead, they set sail intending to make a name for themselves or accomplish something significant, only to find they have drifted off course, sometimes imperceptibly. Leaders and their followers can become lost, adrift in a sea where every course correction seems urgent and important yet never steers them where they need to go. Sometimes the deeper issues of a leader's life can have the same effect on her organization as removing the rudder from a ship: the leader and the organization may move very fast on the surface, but in no particular direction. It is amazing how such drifting can be covered up by focusing on numbers, reorganizing reporting structures, and creating new programs.

Ignoring underlying issues to look good on the surface begins early, through even the most trivial circumstances. Back in grade school, Bruce learned how to hide. While standing in the lunch line one day, he suddenly decided to drop out, giving up his coveted place near the front. The lady behind the counter gave him a peculiar look. A couple of his friends asked him where he was going. Bruce replied, "I'm not really hungry." But this wasn't the whole truth.

You see, Bruce had this weird habit of keeping his lunch money safe by putting it into his mouth. Somewhere in the middle of the lunch line, Bruce had swallowed his lunch money.

Two quarters can't do much to fill a boy's growling belly, but Bruce couldn't bring himself to admit his mistake. Nor could he admit to the peculiar habit of storing his lunch money in his mouth. So he hid the real issues and tried to cover up, going hungry in order to save face. The example of Bruce's predicament may seem juvenile, but people—even those in the most significant roles—make the same kind of choices each day.

Many leaders of corporations, churches, governments, and non-profits hope they can disguise or ignore the underlying issues of their lives—with far more painful outcomes than Bruce suffered. Some may choose to hide their real agendas or weaknesses while pursuing their goals, only to have those issues exposed at an inopportune time. Others may look at the potential dangers of addressing such issues and choose to walk away from influential positions—as if they really could. Walking away from influence is impossible, although we may try to sidestep it.

All of us lead in some respect: as a big sister, a boss, an adviser for a friend, or a role model for our children. And all of us choose whom we will follow. We all participate in the shaping of our own future and produce some degree of inspiration or discouragement in the lives of others. Paul Hersey and Ken Blanchard write that "leadership occurs any time one attempts to influence the behavior of an individual or group, regardless of the reason."[3] So even denying a role or walking away from one has an effect on outcomes and therefore exercises a form of influence. Although we may miss out on leading *well*, clearly none of us can avoid leadership altogether. We all influence others. We can't escape it.

Facing Facts

We also can't escape the facts of our culture. The dawn of this new millennium provides an opportunity to measure the ways the people of the twentieth century affected us. Are we, under their influence, heading full speed ahead toward a disastrous fate? Have we drifted off course?

Marriages and families fall apart. We no longer wonder *if* leaders will fall but rather *when*. The fear of potential litigation haunts every area of life. Our governments add law upon law and build ever larger prisons in the hopes of controlling people who believe they truly cannot control their own actions.

As bleak as this sounds, there is still hope. We can still change course.

This book is for those who want their influence to make a positive difference, in whatever sphere of influence God has granted them. It is for those who wish to explore a better course—one that addresses their inner longings for purpose and meaning. And it is for those who have begun to feel a certain futility in climbing the ladder they have chosen.

The Ascent of a Leader is an invitation to climb a different kind of ladder. This climb beckons you to embrace a lifelong adventure of self-discovery and to couple this adventure with interdependent relationships and perennial pursuit of God. This unique ladder also calls you to create and live within safe environments—to envelop yourself in an ecosystem that awakens and nurtures the purposes God has for you and the people around you. Each human being bears the *imago Dei*, the image of God. *The Ascent of a Leader* speaks to the unique plan and purpose implied by this spark of the divine implanted within you. You have a unique destiny, rooted in who you are, which overflows into all you do and accomplish. Indeed, who you are affects all you do and say, whether who you are reflects the image of God or not. Each task you take on, each relationship you engage in, and each environment you enter can be affected positively by the steps you take now to discover God's purposes for you. A climb of the best kind, this different ladder may scare you at times and cause you to long for safer places while at the same time infusing you with newfound vigor and a pioneering spirit long forgotten.

According to one eyewitness, Captain E. J. Smith attempted to return to the bridge in order to go down with his ship. But while he was climbing a ladder, a wave crashed against him, tearing him away and down into the ocean.

We wonder whether the captain thought, in his last moments, about another ladder—the one he had climbed in order to captain such a majestic ship—and how his choices had brought him to such a fate. Maybe he wondered what could have helped him avoid such an end.

Of all the challenges in life, it is those we discover beneath the surface that will most affect the legacy of our leadership. We encourage you to read on, to face with courage and faith what is presented here. You will not regret it. For it will lead you to a place far above and beyond your own, individual best.

Grabbing Hold

- In the course you have set for your life, how are you providing for the safety of those you influence?
- As you look over your shoulder, who is in the wake of your influence and how are they doing?

Chapter Two

Big Leaders on Short Ladders

It is sometimes frightening to observe the success
which comes even to the outlaw with a polished
technique. . . . But I believe we must reckon with
character in the end, for it is as potent a force in
world conflict as it is in our own domestic affairs. It
strikes the last blow in any battle.

—*Philip D. Reed*

The divorce papers had been served. After many years of marriage, Jim's wife now despised him. He sat alone in the room of an out-of-the-way hotel, ashamed and distraught at the course his life had taken. Even his children held him in contempt. And it seemed they would all be glad when he was gone.

A multimillionaire, Jim felt worthless. At the peak of his career, despair overwhelmed him. He had spent his entire life pursuing what he wanted. But tonight, as he counted the cost, he knew he had lost what he truly needed.

His choices had destroyed all the significant relationships in his life. He thought to himself how much easier it would be simply to end it all rather than to stare this terrifying sense of failure in the face. Just a few pills. Just one pull of the trigger.

How did Jim get to such a place? How does any person who seems so successful on the surface, end up in a place of frustration, anxiety, and even despair? This phenomenon is more common than you may think.

After having conducted extensive research, Dr. J. Robert Clinton, professor of leadership at Fuller Theological Seminary, believes that more than 70 percent of leaders do not finish well. He bases this startling statistic on six criteria, gleaned from common traits among leaders who did not finish well according to their self-analysis, the analysis of their peers and followers, or the teachings of their professed religion. First, leaders who do not finish well lose their learning posture. They stop listening and growing. Second, the attractiveness of their character wanes. Third, they stop living by their convictions. Fourth, they fail to leave behind ultimate contributions. Fifth, they stop walking in an awareness of their influence and destiny. Finally, leaders who finish poorly lose their once vibrant relationship with God.[1]

Many drop out. Most of them plateau (read that as "decline," in our culture of rapid change). And a few need some form of discipline from authorities.[2] Although the media seem to feed on those cases where public correction is needed, the majority of leaders who lose their influence just fade quietly into obscurity.[3] The stories of their lives are written in invisible ink, leaving no mark on history.

Leaders from all walks of life and all types of positions and roles seem equally prone to falling short of becoming who they long to be. What stops them?

Although some cases can be traced to underdeveloped abilities or lack of opportunity, most cannot. The reasons go deeper. As Clinton observes, leaders can do pretty well for themselves through skills alone. "But a leader whose . . . skills outstrip his character formation will eventually falter."[4]

People sense and respond to character almost by intuition. The research of James Kouzes and Barry Posner proves this.[5] Their studies show that we desire leaders who are honest, competent, forward looking, and inspiring—and honesty is the runaway most significant attribute.

Yet fewer than half of us—only 35 percent according to a recent study by the Yale School of Management—believe that our leaders are honest. Why? Sigal Barsad, a professor at Yale and coauthor of the study, summarized people's reasons this way: "People have been hurt."[6] The actions of leaders do not back up their words.

Although many of us recognize and respond negatively to the inconsistency between our leaders' words and deeds, few leaders spend much time deliberately doing anything to become more consistent. Instead, too many leaders spend their energies trying to *appear* more consistent in a superficial way, rather than *becoming* more consistent in a heartfelt, genuine way. This breach between what leaders say and do—between superficiality and genuineness—creates an atmosphere of disillusionment and distrust, germinating a host of organizational and personal ills. Early symptoms, in both leaders and followers, include feeling unfocused, scattered, or overwhelmed. Some sense a growing incongruity between personal and organizational goals. Leaders and managers may grow tired of dealing with difficult or negative individuals, yet they yearn for intimacy and meaningful relationships. Life may feel like a constant reaction to crisis and change. Performance may decline and turnover increase because of apathy and frustration.

Such ills drain our spirits, minds, and bodies, not to mention our families, workplaces, and leisure time. These drains on leadership are far too common. What's worse, many of us live in cultures that seem political, petty, or closed minded. We may lack a safe place to share our concerns or address the causes of our frustration. In some environments, sharing such concerns may lead to greater loss, even separation of some kind or termination. The stress can be felt just as heavily in a home environment as in a Fortune 500 corporation. Is it any wonder leaders fall into severe dysfunction when they sense that no plan or place exists to support them?

Seeds of Destiny

Still, we all want our lives to count, and most of us are not ready to give up. We want to have the ability to change things for the better, to set things right, to be the kind of leaders people look up to. In one way or another, we want to guide our organizations, our families, our friends, or our communities into a better place. That's what the best kind of leadership is about. But how do we get there?

Deep inside each soul, God sows a seed of destiny. The seed starts out small—so small it may go unnoticed or ignored for years. But it is there nonetheless, planted by God to remind us that there is something more to our lives than meets the eye. Just as a vine bears its flowers and then its fruit (and some thorns along the way), so our seed can unfold, following more and more of God's intended plan and purpose for our lives—our destiny.

God uses the totality of our life experiences, both good and bad, to mold and shape each of us uniquely toward specific purposes and goals for our lives. Although God masterfully weaves the strands together, we share responsibility in the process of weaving our destiny. We choose which threads to pull, which colors to highlight. Each decision represents what we believe about ourselves and our world. Each action reveals the fabric of our faith. And each step imprints itself on the tapestry of our own influence—how we will use our authority—and the type of destiny we will ultimately experience.

Some choose rightly. Consequently, their artistry receives appreciation from the crowd. They rise to the top, earning the praise and the trust of others. People look up to them, emulate them, follow them. We call them great leaders. We think of people like Abraham Lincoln, Mother Teresa, and Billy Graham—men and women who would readily admit the insufficiency of the human will or humanistic determination alone in developing extraordinary leadership.

Some choose wrongly. Their influence fades. Instead of a legacy of glory, they earn a legacy of shame. We call them failures or something worse. Yet even some of these have arisen from their ashes, emerging as some of the best leaders.

Most leaders exist somewhere in between, making a mixture of choices—some right, some wrong, and many in assorted shades of gray—struggling to make sense of it all while thirsting for something more.

Leaders and Ladders

During the summers of his university days, Bruce worked for an electrical contractor. Several journeymen enjoyed the twisted thrill of testing his rookie mettle, exposing him to extreme heights, dark tunnels, and shocking experiments. One day, they asked Bruce to climb a too-old ladder truck to install some too-high lights.

Ascending the first extension of rungs posed no problem. But as he continued onto the next extension, connections (and knees) began to wobble. Just before Bruce reached the final rung, the ladder hooks malfunctioned and the extensions collapsed, plummeting him toward earth. Bruce's rapid descent stopped just ten feet short of the ground as the foot of the uppermost ladder extension slammed into the floor of the truck bed. Bruce barely hung on to one of the upper rungs, saving his life. He escaped with a few hand injuries and one more round of veteran-tough laughter from the electrical pros.

Many men and women of influence discover that leadership is like that ladder—a challenging and unpredictable climb, often stable at the bottom and shaky at the top. From the bottom, life at the top looks appealing, even alluring, and many leaders attack the ladder with gusto, confident that they possess what it takes to conquer the rungs.

Yet, when these leaders reach positions of authority, unforeseen instability begins to surface. Such issues as the pressure of success, the temptations of privilege, the demands of followers, and the isolation of leadership leave deep depressions on the rungs—caused by the white-knuckle grip of the leader. Many look for a way to stabilize their situation, but too many leaders come crashing down. And when they land, few are there to help. Some will even laugh.

The Capacity Ladder

Each person has the opportunity to make use of ladders to scale her respective walls. The ladder most are familiar with is one we call the *capacity ladder*. Although capacity ladders come in diverse and sometimes elaborate forms, they all are constructed from the same four basic rungs.

The ascent up the capacity ladder begins with the first rung: *discover what I can do*. (See Figure 2.1.) For instance, when Ken was young, a favorite aunt pointed out and encouraged his ability to draw, and a high school teacher helped him discover his knack for writing. Several of Bill's teachers encouraged his gifts in math and critical thinking. Bruce's entrepreneurial skills expressed themselves early, when he started carnivals, pageants, and student revenue programs. In addition to specific skills, your what-I-can-do inventory may include natural leadership inclinations, a winsome personality,

Figure 2.1. The Rungs of the Capacity Ladder

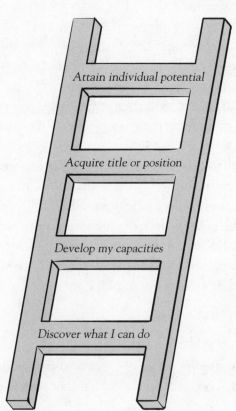

Attain individual potential

Acquire title or position

Develop my capacities

Discover what I can do

a dynamic influence, or an ability to craft a compelling vision or to persuade.

Moving up to the second rung—*develop my capacities*—grants more influence to the leader. At this level, the leader sharpens talents and gifts. Early training often occurs in college and graduate school, and there is further honing during the leader's first engagements with companies, organizations, or religious bodies.

The leader's successful scaling of the first two rungs attracts the attention of executives, administrators, professors, and thousands of group members or constituents who choose their leaders. This attention catapults the person to the third rung, where decision makers and followers *acquire a title or position*. This step up leads naturally to the fourth and final rung: *attain individual potential*. From below, the top rung of the capacity ladder looks great—honor, glory, respect, and power—the results of effective leadership influence.

Is there anything wrong with the rungs on the capacity ladder? Not at all. The desire to aspire to greater challenges and fulfill our potential is a natural part of being human. As beings fashioned in God's image, we have an inborn impulse to better our lives and bring order to our world. When we deny this drive, we become something less than God intended. According to the Bible, God from the very beginning gave humanity the task of tending a garden, and then expanded that task to include caring for the world. Each of us is created with capacities intended for good, no matter how distorted they have become due to our own failures and the failures of others.[7] But the capacity ladder, though necessary, is not sufficient to ensure that our abilities will result in positive influence or an enduring legacy.

Lonely Leaders

After a season or two of influence, many leaders begin to reflect on how they got to the top of the capacity ladder. They remember what they didn't, wouldn't, or couldn't deal with on the way up. But in their present influential position, they assume they cannot talk to others about these things—believing that their present system will not positively reward such disclosure. This creates pressure—a stress felt heaviest at the top of the capacity ladder. "It is lonely at the top," the saying goes, "but you eat better." Most find eating better is not enough.

In environments where the definition of success does not include healthy relationships and character traits like honesty and integrity, leaders may accomplish much but never amount to much, for a very painful reason. It seems the higher leaders climb, the lonelier they become, hiding their true passions and personal challenges from others. Like escaped convicts, they scurry from one hiding place to another, just beyond the teeth of the pursuing hounds. The longer they run from the truth within, the more energy they expend in the attempt to escape themselves. Exhaustion and burnout set in, sometimes to the point that they lose hope altogether.

Sooner or later, many find themselves trapped, like the stag in the Old English poem *Beowulf*. Running from its pursuers, the stag reaches the edge of a lake but, rather than face the dreadful depths, chooses instead to take its chances with the toothy canines:

> *A deer,*
> *Hunted through the woods by packs of Hounds,*
> *A stag with great horns, though driven through the forest*
> *From faraway places, prefers to die*
> *On those shores, refuses to save its life*
> *In that water*[8]

Have you ever known someone like this? Someone who has refused to dive into the deeper things? Someone who has all the capacity-ladder rungs in place and reaps the benefits of having attained individual accomplishments—yet you sense something wrong? Talent, gift, and performance shine in these people. Like the stag with great horns, they seem strong, beautiful, and proud. But immaturity in character tarnishes their influence, usually doing them in.

Usually it is relational problems that expose this character immaturity. When leaders with undeveloped character rise up the capacity ladder, their actions have a negative impact on those around them, and these relationship issues can sap the strength of leaders and their followers like a viral infection. Friendships become fragmented and superficial. Immature leaders may manipulate or deceive followers, wounding them in the process. Instead of admitting their mistakes, they may try to cover them up, becoming even more isolated. Leaders who neglect the development of their inner world feel threatened by those who challenge them. They view power as a means to dominate others. Such leaders undervalue others and overvalue themselves. All of this wreaks havoc in relationships, unmasking the leader's character immaturity.

Even at the top of the capacity ladder, leaders may not have begun to address the disconnect between the development of their character and the development of their capacities. This character gap creates big leaders on short ladders—when undeveloped, immature motives and values negatively affect even the best of capacities. The guy wires of privilege and power cannot steady the relational problems this circumstance causes. Stephen Covey came to the same conclusion when he wrote, "Many people with secondary greatness—that is, social recognition for their talents—lack primary greatness or goodness in their character. Sooner or later, you'll see this in every long-term relationship they have, whether it is with a business associate, a spouse, a friend or a teenage child going through an identity crisis."[9]

Redefining Success

According to Kouzes and Posner, "Managers get other people to do, but leaders get other people to *want* to do. Leaders do this by first of all being credible. That is the foundation for all leadership."[10] But think on this: What gets the leader at the top of the capacity ladder to *want* to lead this way—getting other people to *want to do*—especially when simply getting people to *do* has immediate, tangible benefits? For instance, what makes a person want to be credible when a white lie obtains the desired result? Certainly the benefits of being trusted or the pitfalls of being caught would help persuade a leader to do the right thing. But when weighed against the privileges of power, position, and wealth, such benefits and pitfalls seem to take a seat at the back of the bus, close to the emergency exit.

On the capacity ladder, many emerging or reemerging leaders do whatever it takes within their organization to reach a position of influence and to stay there. They call this success.

Years ago, during the Second World War, *Life* magazine carried a full-page picture of Avery Sewell, the one-time Montgomery Ward corporate tycoon, in a rather embarrassing pose. Apparently Sewell, sensing that things might not go well after the war, hoarded large sums of inventory and funds to protect himself and his organization from insolvency. The government did not appreciate this practice and warned him several times to cease and desist. He did not, so the board itself finally voted Sewell out of the chairmanship. However, Sewell refused to step down, and the *Life* cover portrays the chairman, still sitting in his leadership chair, being carried out by federal police officers and placed on the sidewalk outside headquarters.

Is this phenomenon new? Not at all. Read the gospel stories in the Bible, and you will notice that a dispute arose among several of Jesus' hand-picked leaders as to which of them would occupy the top rung.[11] The desire to aspire inappropriately is as old as time and as current as our own hearts. We all face the possibility of becoming big leaders on short ladders.

People who trust and follow such leaders eventually pay for their trust, sometimes with tragic results. Why do they follow? Because followers see the strength of personality (rung one), benefit from the leader's developed gifts (rung two), place confidence in the leader's office or position (rung three), and assume . . . what? The leader's emotional, spiritual, and relational maturity. Needy people are especially susceptible to this misplaced trust. And leaders without character are especially *tempted* by their followers' misplaced trust.

Starting Over

Whereas for some leaders a fall from the top exposes their inner failures, for others failure means staying at the top. For these folks, failure means living with an intimate awareness of an inner cancer that eats away at their very being, reminding them daily that something is wrong. In such cases, a fall may come as a relief, forming the basis for a welcome fresh start. Thankfully, that's what happened to Jim, the man whose story began this chapter.

Eight years after the scene in the hotel, Jim took the podium at a business luncheon. He told stories of his past pursuits, the rights he had won, and his rise to power. He captured everyone's attention when he told of selling his privately owned company for $400 million. But the real story began as he described the ultimate impact of his past choices, culminating that night when he hid in the hotel room, contemplating suicide.

Something died that night. Not Jim's body, of course, but a growth deep inside his heart. His dogged pursuit of power suffered a lethal dose of radiation, and the stranglehold money had on his heart began to loosen. Jim's influence didn't decrease after his experience: it began to expand. The financial rewards of his business blossomed. But instead of becoming a slave to his increased success, he began to give of himself and his money in increasing measure to worthy causes. Jim finished his speech by challenging other businesspeople to do the same.

Jim had been a leader from his youth. But now, somehow, his leadership had been altered in a way that benefited others while nourishing his own heart and soul. He had found a different path. Where? And how? What made the difference in his character, relationships, and influence? The answer couldn't be found in his abilities and capacities. It couldn't be found in his position of power and authority. In fact, his bondage to these very things almost destroyed him. Jim almost lost it all before reevaluating his path. But he did alter his path.

You may have trusted leaders who let you down. You may be a successful leader at the top of a capacity ladder that is beginning to feel unstable. You may be a leader who has fallen off the capacity ladder or who yearns to avoid such a fall. You may be an emerging leader in a business, company, school, organization, or church, wondering why the development of your inner life has not kept pace with the development of your capacity.

If so, read on as we present the time-tested process of intentionally ascending a different kind of ladder. It too has its privileges. It too leads to influence. It too produces results. But of a very different nature.

Grabbing Hold

- Who benefits from your success?
- In setting direction, are you reacting to circumstances, or acting on convictions?
- If climbing the capacity ladder does not fulfill you, what will?
- What benefits have you gained from those who most influenced you?

Chapter Three

Creating Environments That Uphold and Empower Us

If you want to build a ship, don't drum up the men
to gather wood, divide the work, and give orders.
Instead, teach them to yearn for the vast and
endless sea.

—*Antoine de Saint Exupéry*

A few years ago, a leader came to us with a problem. Recently promoted to head the U.S. division of a large international enterprise, he spent his first few weeks sizing up the state of the organization and his team of several dozen seasoned leaders. Although he had inherited a talented team, they had reached a plateau. They fulfilled their job descriptions, but they couldn't seem to get to the next level. An invisible barrier held them back. You could actually feel the sense of stagnation.

The new head needed to act quickly, because key leaders were becoming discouraged. But how do you correct something as slippery as a "feeling"? He didn't want to change the mission. It was a great mission. He could not correct the problem through greater accountability, restructuring, or any of the latest leadership development techniques. Many past attempts at fixing things just seemed to contribute more to the slump. To find a solution, he had to go below the surface and analyze the roots of their corporate culture.

At a national meeting, he praised his team for their accomplishments and commitment, and reminded them of the deep heritage and value of their mission. Then he went further, explaining how their mission was now jeopardized by a lack of authenticity within their ranks. Obsessive accountability had encouraged them to hide the truth about themselves and their jobs from each other. Their fear of losing position or status had bred isolation, inauthentic relationships, and, for some, feelings of bitterness, jealousy, and contempt. Rigid divisions of labor and excessive competitiveness had robbed them of creativity and fun. On the surface, things always appeared fine—as they must, if decorum was to be maintained. But underneath, a cauldron boiled, slowly poisoning their hearts with its vapors. It was time for a wholesale change.

They needed to create an environment where people sensed enough safety to be real. They needed an atmosphere where people could breathe with integrity, where they felt trusted and valued for who they really were. The time for hiding behind stereotypes and false facades needed to come to an end, or in addition to losing good people, they would soon lose their ability to fulfill their mission.

After the meeting, the new leader acknowledged to us that he wasn't sure how to make such an environmental change. His observations and questions deeply challenged us. Was such a fundamental cultural change possible? How?

The dynamics of culture can elevate people and organizations or weigh them down. The privilege and responsibility to nurture and release individual and organizational potential rests squarely on the shoulders of leaders. Therefore, to motivate change and growth, leaders must master the dynamics of culture. As Edgar Schein observes, "Neither culture nor leadership . . . can really be understood by itself. In fact, one could argue that the only thing of real importance that leaders do is create and manage culture and the unique talent of leaders is their ability to understand and work with culture."[1] The ability to initiate and sustain positive cultural changes may prove to be the single greatest need of twenty-first-century organizations.

Culture does not function according to mechanical principles. According to Schein's model, every culture has artifacts (outcomes we see and measure), espoused values (what we say about who we are and what we do), and a third, harder to manage element he calls underlying assumptions.[2] If culture could be managed by stating desired outcomes, we could achieve our goals by simply changing our set of espoused values. For instance, if we want our kids to behave, we could post a set of rules on the fridge with a list of corresponding forms of discipline for disobedience. Or, if we want people to be honest, we could add a corporate value statement that says, "We will be honest with each other and terminate those we catch in dishonest acts." But as any parent or supervisor knows, these methods won't work.

Cultural change requires more systemic medicine than the topical ointment of changing espoused values. That's why drugs still pervade "drug-free" school zones. That's why deception and fraud still thrive in governments founded on the rule of law. That's why behavior-based training, when not integrated with who we are, loses its potency as soon as competition or crisis arises. Bringing what we *actually* do into full alignment with what we *say* we want to do requires us to look deeper. We must explore the underlying assumptions about who we are. Positive cultural change means removing the barriers between what is good within our own souls and what is good within the soul of the cultures we live in.

Removing Barriers to Trust

Frank Brock once faced this challenge when he took over as CEO of his family business. He inherited a candy-making enterprise with declining profits, eroding market share, and very low morale. Though armed with a Harvard degree and recent military leadership experience, he felt ill-prepared for such a challenge. Brock had a couple options. He could carry on business as usual, making small but honorable efforts until the company slid into obscurity, or he could begin to rewrite the company's recipe for success from scratch. But how? He had no idea. He thought to himself: shouldn't a new CEO have answers? Isn't that what everyone expects?

Brock made a choice that many in leadership find difficult. He called a series of meetings with people from the plant floor and started asking *them* the questions: "What are we doing wrong? What needs to change?" At first, the plant workers questioned his motives. Nothing like this had ever happened before, so their suspicions kept their lips tightly sealed. But after Brock repeatedly assured them of his sincerity and promised to protect them from any backlash, a few, including Evelyn, the chief baker, finally took the risk and spoke up:

> "If you want to know what's wrong with the candy, Mr. Brock, just ask one of my kids. They'll tell you there's more scrap in the bag than there is whole candy. That crazy German ordered us to throw some of the crushed candy scraps into every bag to get the weight up," Evelyn reported, referring to Brock's autocratic and immensely unpopular predecessor.
>
> "If you want to know why Brock candy ain't sellin', that's it. Or at least part of it," observed Delmer, a key operator on the assembly line.
>
> "That will be changed. Today!" Frank declared. "Now what else do I need to know?"[3]

What Brock began that day steamrolled. More and more workers opened up as they learned that the boss not only listened to their ideas but actually followed through on them. The workers on the plant floor could make a real difference. Their suggestions ultimately led to the design and construction of a new factory, built to *employee* specifications. But it didn't end there. Brock went further, becoming involved in the personal lives of his employees as well, even to the point of making sure one family had running water installed in their backwoods home.

Our hearts vibrate when we hear stories like this one; something quickens deep within. We want this kind of leadership. We want to be leaders like that. But we may identify more with the first leader, who felt unsure that things could really change after years of positive reinforcement of negative habits. Both stories reflect the significant impact an environment can have on people's

hearts. Both stories reflect a tremendous struggle most le
whether in the home, the church, or the workplace: hov
the kind of environment where individuals can soar above and beyond their best.

Bill Pollard, chairman of ServiceMaster, tells us, "In the absence
of grace, there will be no reaching for potential."[4] He is right. Life
is full of possibilities, but each comes laden with risks. To take risks,
we need to feel a certain degree of safety and security in our environment. We lose hope when we sense no room for the occasional
misstep or setback. Without hope, we cease to dream about possibilities. To take risks, to hope despite setbacks, and to dream about
better tomorrows requires grace. Without grace, life is bleak indeed.
But what does such grace mean, practically?

Environments of Grace

Though you may never have studied grace in sociology class, we can
look at grace from a sociological perspective. As we relate to each
other in social contexts, grace means we show unmerited concern
and favor to each other. Like the bishop in the classic tale *Les Mis-
érables*, we may even turn our most treasured possessions over to
those like Jean Valjean—vagrant convicts who cheat us, steal from
us, and lie to us—caught red-handed. Grace means people don't get
what they deserve. It means we treat each other better than we expect to be treated ourselves. Grace transcends justice. We meet a
need expecting nothing in return. We forgive. We pay back insults
with concern, as the reformed Valjean did when he took in a dying
prostitute who had spat in his face, then went further by promising
to care for her orphaned daughter, Cosette. Actions like these represent grace in action, person to person.

Grace begets grace. Trace an act of grace back to its roots, and
you will find that ultimately its source is God. Follow an act of grace
to its conclusion, and you will find that eventually it leads people
back to God. For instance, the bishop received grace from God and
passed it on to the mendicant Valjean. As a result, Valjean soon

found God. Valjean received the grace God offered to him and passed it on to a desperate woman trapped in prostitution. The woman soon found God. The unmerited favor of God, when transferred through human acts of unmerited favor, transforms even the most hardened hearts. Selfish, hedonistic, and stubborn people become people who selflessly, sacrificially, and mercifully extend the same grace to others. Though grace may be discussed most often in theology classes, grace certainly has sociological implications.

If grace can be viewed from a sociological perspective, can we also look at it from a meteorological perspective? Can we gauge an environment of grace, like the weatherpeople predict sunshine or rain? Maybe it sounds like we're reaching here, but bear with us.

Most people know an environment of grace when they see it. They simply point to the results: people feel safe, they grow up, they trust each other, they live authentically, they celebrate each other, they laugh a lot, they produce better. But in some environments, grace is so evident you can feel it from the first, even prior to a cognitive understanding of observed behaviors. For example, wherever Dr. Gerald May of the Shalem Institute finds communities where people successfully combat destructive addictions, he feels such an environment. "Its power includes not just love that comes from people and through people, but love that pours forth among people, as if through the very spaces between one person and the next. Just to be in such an atmosphere is to be bathed in healing power."[5]

This may sound a bit esoteric, but it's not unlike describing any environmental condition. When someone asks you how the weather is, you may say it's invigorating—the sky is blue, the sun is warm, and the air is clear and fresh. You probably won't say that particles in the atmosphere are reflecting a blue tint due to cooler, moist air caused by recent precipitation in the higher altitudes. And if you did say that, someone more qualified would have a more accurate explanation.

Although too few leaders can accurately describe the principles and processes for cultivating an environment of grace (a benefit we hope you receive by reading this book), the results are clear. People feel empowered. They sense that who they are is OK, even though they know greater things are expected of them. They perceive the freedom to make important contributions, even when their suggestions require significant changes or their questions test long-held assumptions. They discern a positive spirit that acts as a catalyst in their soul, giving them a sense of hope that "here is a place where I belong." This is home. Where can we find such environments?

Taking Hold of the Rails

To find or create environments of grace, we need to climb a different kind of ladder. This ladder can be distinguished from the capacity ladder in a number of ways.

First of all, it has more rungs—five instead of four—so it's naturally longer. In the chapters that follow, we will discuss each of its five rungs in detail. This ladder could go by a number of names because it produces a multitude of powerful benefits. It could be called the ladder of promise, the ladder of grace, the ladder of relationships, or even the ladder of destiny. Because the rungs of this ladder represent principles that can help people intentionally develop character, we will call it the character ladder.

Second, the character ladder requires a great deal more personal and organizational investment than its shorter sibling—investments that pay rich dividends. We'll point out these costs and dividends as we move up the rungs.

Third, the character ladder has longer and stronger *rails*. Here the differences between the character and capacity ladders begin to be keenly felt. On both the character ladder and the capacity ladder, one rail represents environment and the other rail represents relationships. Environment and relationships are two sides of the same coin, or, in our metaphor, two rails on the same ladder. Developing healthy relationships in an unhealthy environment is nearly impossible, as is constructing a positive environment with a group of negative people. You can't climb any ladder with one rail missing, including the character ladder. Figure 3.1. illustrates the rails of the character ladder.

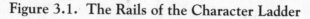

Figure 3.1. The Rails of the Character Ladder

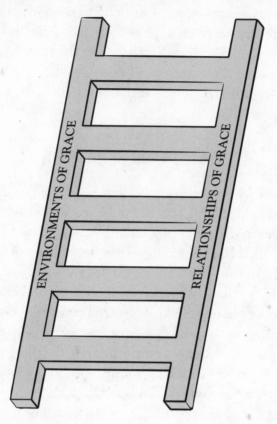

An environment of grace works hand in hand with relationships of grace to create cultures in which trust, creativity, hope, and other positive outcomes emerge. Leadership sage Chris Argyris also observed this parallel: "Without interpersonal competence or a 'psychologically safe' environment, the organization is a breeding ground for mistrust, intergroup conflict, rigidity and so on, which lead to a decrease in organizational success in problem solving."[6] The right relationships without the right environment will not last long, and vice versa.

Because environment affects our relationships and relationships affect environment, we may wonder how to distinguish between the two rails. Environment includes things like organizational style, sentiments, expectations, and certain artifacts. Are there photos and mementos hanging on the walls? What are they saying? Can I wear sandals here, or do I need a tie? If the boss' shirt is buttoned wrong, does anyone tell him? Can I laugh out loud, or does everyone whisper? Do people watch the clock? Do they watch each other? Does gender or race or marital status matter? Are there celebrations of successes, transitions, or milestones? Does excellence matter? Do I matter? These things can be experienced without forming personal relationships, yet they provide the context for relational health or dysfunction. Environment can repel us or draw us in. It can open us up or shut us down.

The late H. R. Rookmaaker, professor at the Free University of Amsterdam, identified music as a key player in environment, a kind of tuning fork by which we determine whether we can harmonize with those around us. "Music we have around us forms part of our environment and our lifestyle, that is, ourselves," he said. He pointed out the inverse as well: just as environment can mold us, "the environment that we create is something that goes out of us."[7] We are not simply products of our environment. Our environments are also a product of us.

Just as the outcomes of an environment of grace can be clearly seen, so can those of an environment lacking grace, or as the writer Philip Yancey calls it, ungrace. Argyris pointed out some of these ungracious outcomes: mistrust, conflict, rigidity, and decreased problem-solving abilities—and there are others. In an atmosphere of ungrace, all favor and love must be earned. When humans, who all fall short, feel they cannot earn favor or love without meeting a too-high standard, they lose hope. Or they put their hope in their ability to pretend that they have no frailties or weaknesses, at least long enough to get to the top of the capacity ladder.

In their book, *Encouraging the Heart*, Kouzes and Posner describe three effects of a leadership style that encourages an environment of ungrace: "First, people get a distorted view of reality. Second, over time production declines. Third, the manager's personal credibility hits bottom."[8] How does this occur? Kouzes and Posner continue, "If you knew someone was coming around to check up on you, how would you behave? As soon as you spot the boss coming, you put on your best behavior. Actually, we may put on *different* behavior, but it's not our *best*. In fact, it can be our worst. Why? Because we get nervous and tense, and when we're nervous and tense we slip up more. The manager who wanders around with an eye out for trouble is more likely to get just that: more trouble."[9]

Principles, Relationships, and Environments

To break the cycle of an environment of ungrace, we must explore and address what Schein calls the "underlying assumptions" of culture. The capacity and character ladders have fundamentally different underlying assumptions, which naturally lead to different values and outcomes, including environmental change. We suggest there are three basic components that interact to create cultural change at the deepest level: principles, relationships, and environments. Each component has its importance. But none of the components can succeed on its own.

We can teach new principles, but unless they flesh themselves out in meaningful, daily interaction with others, they can turn into stale dogma or even into ungracious rules and regulations—the exact opposite of their intent. We can say we're about building relationships, but unless we have a supportive environment and principles to govern them, we will fall back into old patterns of isolation and loneliness, just faking it with more people than we did before.

This presents a dilemma for leaders: where do we begin the process of cultural change? It seems logical to start with principles, move to application in relationships, then hope for an environment to emerge. While this may sound logical and linear to a leader attempting to foster change, individuals rarely respond in such a planned fashion. Instead, they seem to embrace change from the opposite direction. First, they intuit the environment, feeling for a sense of safety and affinity before they enter into more intimate relationships. And only after relationships begin to "work" for them will they begin to understand, articulate, and espouse the underlying principles behind the process they have been through.

Most often, it seems that all three components interplay with one another. A new relationship will spark a new understanding of principle amid a supportive environment. A new principle will spark a new environment amid a supportive relationship. The three components work in a symbiotic, circular dependence, where none can thrive without the other. (See Figure 3.2.)

Misunderstanding the dynamic interplay of principles, relationships, and environment can lead to some misguided initiatives. For instance, an organization may decide to write or purchase computer software for time management and then distribute that software to every staff person, requiring everyone to record how much time is spent each day in certain activities. Headquarters would

Figure 3.2. The Interdependence of Environment, Relationships, and Principles

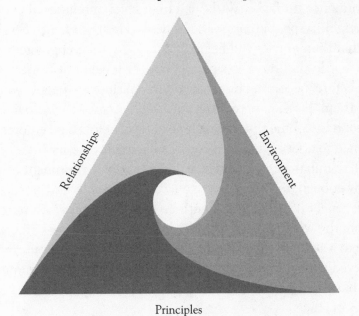

Principles

then collect all the data and measure each staff person against pre-determined quotas thought to represent positive character traits. Ul-timately, it is assumed, the software and resulting analysis should lead to better character and an environment that nurtures character.

In a culture that values measurement, performance standards, discipline, and technology that fosters "objective" analysis, such a plan may make sense. The underlying assumptions probably include a belief that conformity to a "good" system implies "good" charac-ter. The leaders presume that their staff are honest in using the soft-ware, no matter what the repercussions. In fact, they probably take it for granted that their people have enough character to use the software in a way that achieves character!

There's nothing wrong with using good time-management soft-ware. But using it to launch a character-development program into a culture lacking the environment, relationships, and principles to support character development is about as useful as a snowmobile in the Sahara desert.

Why doesn't it work? In an environment of ungrace, end users assume that the software represents another method of enforcing performance for favor. Without a high level of relational trust and vulnerability, people cannot be honest about their faults. So know-ing that their entries will be used to measure their character perfor-mance, the staff have to sink to a deeper level of dishonesty than ever before, becoming more isolated from the very people who can help them. Further, no matter how well designed the software is, it is wrong to assume that character can be developed by enforced ad-herence to a set of rules or performance requirements.

To climb the character ladder, we need an environment of grace. Oddly enough, the very places you would expect to find grace, many times reflect it the least. Sometimes religious organizations manu-facture the worst kind of capacity ladders by requiring strict adher-ence to a set of do's and don'ts in order to be accepted, affirmed, or received with respect, dignity, and honor. But faith communities also have the potential to be the most profound examples of en-claves of grace.

When our friend Wendy first experienced an environment of grace, she didn't enjoy it very much. A successful stock broker eyeing a political career, Wendy had enjoyed a charmed life as the well-loved, well-educated, well-adjusted child of a wonderfully functional family. One Sunday, at the suggestion of her husband, Wendy visited a new church. At least that's what her husband called it.

To Wendy, a bunch of people wearing anything from suits to shorts and sandals, a preacher wearing chinos and sneakers, and a "choir" consisting of a "four-piece rock band with four 'back-up chicks'" did not seem anything like a real church. What was worse, she embarrassed herself by laughing out loud with everyone else during the preacher's sermon. But by the time the sermon ended, tears streaked her cheeks. Something deep inside her had been touched.

She tried to bolt for the car as soon as the service ended, but was stopped by an old high school friend who used to be "the consummate bad boy," who greeted her with a broad smile and said, "Isn't this place great?"

"What happened to him?" she wondered as she pressed on to the parking lot. In the car, her husband asked her what she thought of the place. Wendy replied, "I hated it!"

"I thought so," her husband replied, "but would you consider giving it another try?"

"I can't believe I'm saying this," Wendy answered, "but I think we have to go back. I don't know why, but I felt something in there that I've never felt before. I don't want to, but I know I have to go back."

Wendy did go back. Several years earlier Wendy's husband had contracted cancer. Then her first-born daughter almost died from a severe neurological illness. Shortly after settling into the church, Wendy's doctors diagnosed a life-threatening complication during her third pregnancy—for her and the baby. Things seemed to be crumbling all around her. What happened to that perfect, predictable, and productive life?

Wendy and her family needed help. The environment at that church gave her the strength she needed to risk asking for help. Because she felt unmerited favor, she could openly ask hard questions about suffering without fear of belittlement. Because she found safety, she could express her sorrow and grief. In this environment, she could risk admitting her needs, without fearing loss of respect for her abilities and potential. The people at the church responded to her needs with listening ears and helping hands. Please don't miss this point. It was the environment that melted away Wendy's resistance to receiving the care of others. The fact that she found such a climate at a church is not the point. The truth is, far too few churches possess such an environment, regardless of their stated doctrinal commitments to grace.

Environments of grace can also appear in the most unlikely places, like Silicon Valley. Rick McEachern, senior marketing manager at Apple Computer, suggests that environment "set the tone" for Apple's return to fiscal health and prominence in the computing world of the late nineties.[10]

Whatever one thinks of Steve Jobs, he demonstrated excellent leadership when he returned to Apple. One of the first things he did was to consolidate staff from a variety of scattered buildings into a newly constructed campus. On this campus, you can go to work in a suit or jeans. You can wear your hair long or shave it off. You can hold a meeting in a coffee bar, a gymnasium, or a comfy conference room full of toys. In short, you are encouraged to be yourself. In addition, you are always part of a team that cannot accomplish its goal without you. And everyone is connected by e-mail, phone, or pager at all times. Why?

Because we—even those who design and build machines— don't function like machines. We need an environment where we sense the freedom to be who we are, within boundaries framed by values and a common goal. We need to feel we are safe and supported as whole people who have significant things to contribute, despite our differences. We need to be creative. And we need to communicate with all kinds of people who have information we do not, because none of us knows everything. We need each other. And we need an environment around us that acknowledges and supports these facts.

Jobs may or may not understand the underpinnings or ultimate source of grace, but he constructed a physical environment that spoke unmerited favor into the lives of Apple employees. He didn't have to do this to get computers designed and built. But according to McEachern, you can actually feel the difference on the campus. People actually believe they can create "insanely great" products again. And they are! Their response to Jobs's environmental sensitivity may have, at least in part, saved the company from certain demise.

Of course, you may say, Jobs is no ordinary person, and he was handed an extraordinary opportunity few of us will ever encounter. Maybe. But the same principles apply in the most humble circumstances. When leaders create an atmosphere of care and concern, hope and vision flourish. The seeds of destiny in their followers begin to crack through their shells as leaders encourage each person with the prospect of becoming all they are intended to be. But tough choices need to be made, not just organizational choices, but personal ones. Can we set aside a solely personal agenda to benefit others? Can we accept people who look, act, and even believe differently than we believe if we know it will release their potential? This doesn't mean we just tolerate them; it means we extend unmerited favor to them, namely grace. Can we admit our own frailties, declare our own strengths, and receive the strengths of others despite their weaknesses? Can we examine whether our expectations of others do more to reinforce our personal biases than to release others into who God created them to be?

How can we make such choices in our own lives? How can we open ourselves up to the possibilities of an environment of grace when we may not be experiencing an environment of grace ourselves? We may say, "It's just not that simple!"

Actually, at the risk of sounding trite, it is that simple. As leaders of families, organizations, and other groups, we are responsible for creating the environments we live and work in. It is our choices that determine the course of culture. We cannot merely fall back on excuses when we are the "they" who make the rules and model how to live by them. If we long for true empowerment, if we aspire to trust others and be trusted, if we know the productivity and joy of working in environments of grace, the first move is ours. Or is it?

You see, we all need an environment of grace. And for us to make that first move, we must realize that we also have been influenced by our environments, whether we created them or not. And the first move may already have been made by someone else in our past. Do you know or have you experienced an environment of grace? Have you tasted it? Perhaps you felt it around a mentor. Maybe you perceived it at home, at church, or among a special group of friends. Remember what it was like? Remember the impact it had on you? To make the first move, we need to find or return to those kinds of environments for the support we need. We cannot transfer to others what we do not know and experience ourselves any more than we can come back from where we have not been. We'll share more on this in later chapters.

If we look at the task of leading a group or company as though it were the task of building a ship in order to set sail, perhaps we could say that during the twentieth century leaders have invested too much in figuring out how better to gather wood and divide the work and give orders. Maybe leaders should have been teaching people to yearn for the vast and endless sea. Possibilities fill that vast and endless sea. An environment of grace supplies the strength, encouragement, and creativity we need to prepare our ship for such an adventure. When we do cast off together, an environment of grace will put the wind in our sails. It replenishes our stores with hope. It enlivens the decks with encouragement. An environment of grace gives the families, groups, and organizations we lead a fighting chance of completing the journey as planned, despite setbacks. Our yearnings find answers when we live and work together in such an environment.

Environment represents one rail of the ladder. The other rail is relationships, and it is to this rail that we will turn our attention next.

Grabbing Hold

- How does the level of emotional safety in your work environment affect your contribution?
- Do you think the risks of building relationships are worth the rewards?
- In your current work, worship, and home environments, can you identify some of the underlying assumptions that affect those environments?
- What one environment can you begin to have an impact on today?

Chapter Four

Nurturing Relationships That Ground and Sustain Us

We are all angels with only one wing; we can only
fly while embracing one another.
—*Luciano De Crescenzo*

Back in the early 1930s, Elton Mayo of Harvard University drew some groundbreaking conclusions from experiments at a Western Electric plant in Hawthorne, Illinois. Tests had already been conducted to determine the effects of lighting on a control group and a test group. As expected, when the lighting on the factory floor increased, so did the productivity of the test group. But something strange happened. The productivity of the control group rose as well, even though their lighting had not changed.

So they called in Mayo and his team, who expanded the testing by giving special perks, such as rest breaks and free lunches, to a test group of women who assembled telephone relays. They gave no perks to a similar control group. Again, the productivity of *both* groups went up. Bewildered, they decided to take away everything and return the women to their original work conditions. This produced astounding results: productivity in both groups reached an all-time high! The reasons?

Paul Hersey and Kenneth Blanchard summarize what Mayo found after conducting interviews with the women: "As a result of the attention lavished upon them by experimenters, the women felt they were an important part of the company. They no longer viewed themselves as isolated individuals, working together only in the sense that they were physically close to each other. Instead, they

43

had become members of a congenial, cohesive workgroup. The relationships that developed elicited feelings of affiliation, competence, and achievement. These needs, which had long gone unsatisfied at the workplace, were now being fulfilled."[1]

Mayo's research and studies by those who followed in his footsteps determined that "the most significant factor affecting organizational productivity was . . . interpersonal relationships that are developed on the job."[2] To be sure, the environment at Hawthorne triggered those changes in relationships, though in a backhanded way. If the women at the plant had not felt the affirmation and acceptance that came from all the attention, they would probably have remained as isolated as before.

The Importance of Needs

Studies like these emphasize an age-old truth that helps explain why leaders malfunction while climbing the capacity ladder: every one of us has needs that can only be met by God and others.[3] A need is anything we require or lack, in order to be fulfilled and productive. Like the women on the plant floor, we have a need for attention. We also have needs for significance, for protection, for security, and for provision. And there are many others. Because these needs can seem so "soft," they may not attract attention. But when we deny our God-given needs, try to meet them on our own, or demand that others meet them on our terms, we will not experience fulfillment. Without fulfillment—the realization of our abilities and potential—we will not only accomplish less, but will also fall far short of the greater purposes for our lives.

Yet many still bet against this truth, clinging to their isolation for fulfillment. In the classic tale *The Great Divorce*, C. S. Lewis illustrates this point as he wryly recounts a wild bus ride from hell to heaven. Instead of finding fire in hell, Lewis discovered street after street of rather nice homes, but all had been abandoned. Lewis asked an educated man, "Was there once a much larger population?" His response sent chills down Lewis's spine, even aboard the hot bus:

Not at all. The trouble is that they're so quarrelsome. As soon as anyone arrives he settles in some street. Before he's been there twenty-four hours he quarrels with his neighbor. Before the week is over he's quarreled so badly that he decides to move. Very likely he finds the next street empty 'cause all the people there have quarreled with *their* neighbors—and moved. So he settles in. If by any chance the street is full, he goes further. But even if he stays, it makes no odds. He's sure to have another quarrel pretty soon and then he'll move on again. Finally, he'll move right to the edge of town and build a new house. You see, it's easy here. You've only got to *think* a house and there it is. That's how the town keeps on growing.[4]

The Problem with Pursuing Rights

What a haunting picture. Yet all of us can relate to this tendency to avoid the potential risks associated with interdependence. When given the choice to stick it out through the tough times or to run, most of us would rather run from relationships, trying to find an easier way to get what we want. We tend to choose isolation over community.

On the capacity ladder, might makes right. We're told that nice people finish last and that the end justifies the means. The utilitarian nature of capacity-ladder relationships makes the ladder quite portable. As Figure 4.1 illustrates, when relationships get tough, we can fold up the ladder, pack it away, and move it to another location, but the people stay behind. And we keep getting more and more lonely as our families, organizations, and cultures fragment. To avoid such a hell on earth, we must acknowledge our hubris and our needs and understand the process of meeting those needs.

When relationships become expendable and expedient—used for gain and then left behind—the relationship rail becomes very weak and fragile, because such relationships deny the time-intensive process necessary for the meeting of needs. All too often, relationships on the capacity ladder turn into a pursuit of personal power *over* others, evidenced by a constant battle for individual or special

Figure 4.1. The Portable Capacity Ladder

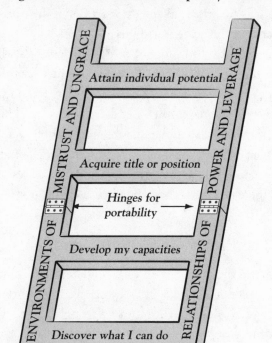

rights. Pursuing power over others increases isolation, inhibiting character development. Manipulative, contrived connections may help us acquire certain rights, but they cannot meet our deepest needs. These needs can only be met by the gracious care and concern of others—the kind we cannot buy, demand, or extract through power over others.

Created for Community

Many organizations claim to be organized in teams these days. This is a good trend. But teams will become an endangered species unless we stop isolated people from destroying the habitat they need to survive. We must keep the purpose and potential of teams in plain view. Teams work best when there is a mutual acknowledgment that each member needs the others, not just to perform a task but to experience personal fulfillment.

Intellectually, we may understand these words. But do we know them experientially? There are many leaders who could write this chapter but who live a mechanical, isolated, unsatisfying existence.

Teams must go beyond the mechanics of task and function. We each have deeper needs that must be met in relationships—at home, at church, and even at work—in order for us to experience fulfillment. Every relationship has the potential to provide something we need. And every relationship has a purpose for us—to meet someone else's need.

We meet needs in others through expressions of our love. For example, when we listen, we meet someone's need for attention. When we affirm, we meet someone's need for significance. When we protect, we meet someone's need for security, and so on. We may demand the right to protection or affirmation or security, but we are fulfilled only when love comes to us in grace, in the context of un-merited favor.

How insightful of Lewis to point out that the continuously divorcing inhabitants of hell could get anything they wanted by simply wishing it. Under such conditions, what needs would stimulate them to cooperate? When these people believed they could survive without stores, streets, museums, or love, relationships became obsolete. Thankfully, we don't live there. Affluence, power, or privilege may deceive us into believing the lie of self-sufficiency for awhile, but our yearning for fulfillment still prods us in the direction we must go—toward community. Here, in this reality, we still have itches in the middle of our backs that can only be scratched by someone else.

Bob Buford, owner of a cable television company and founder of Leadership Network, acknowledged how we sometimes stumble toward community when he wrote, "I have never done anything important outside the context of team. I think God must laugh at the seeming independence of us human beings who have such a tendency toward hubris and self-sufficiency. This may come from having made a lot of money, earning acclaim in sports, writing a book or accomplishing something else extraordinary. God finds ways to teach all of us who are puffed up with ourselves how inter-dependent we really are."[5]

This meeting of needs is really the process of love. The process of love is a highly individualized thing. Each of us best expresses our care for others in different ways. Thus we hear individual callings passed on from the Caller. One teaches. Another heals. Some ad-ministrate and others possess a particular capacity to give or to serve. Community relationships function like a body, with a whole bunch of individual parts that must function in harmony with oth-ers.[6] We experience the deepest fulfillment when we receive attrib-utes of love that meet our needs and then reciprocate, reflecting our concern back onto others according to our calling and gifts.

Some call this the soft side of leadership. But the benefits are far from soft. When we sense a freedom to express our care and con-cern for others according to the unique way God has created us, everyone benefits. We experience the hope of fulfilling our particu-lar purpose and destiny within the only context that can sustain our pursuit—community. And we recognize our larger purpose within the whole, to influence others, in love, as they seek to fulfill their unique role in that same context.

Still, this may sound a little touchy-feely for some. So let's get very practical and specific.

Needs, Love, and the Bottom Line

Anne Wilson Shaef and Diane Fassel collaborated on a work titled *The Addictive Organization*, in which they exposed the dangers of unhealthy organizational environments. In one of their studies they followed the changes in the cardiac unit of a teaching hospital. The hospital had decided to admit six cardiology residents each year, with the intention of eliminating three as the year progressed. This created an environment in which workaholism, stress, fierce competition, and isolation thrived. In order to hold their position, the residents would not allow themselves to be outdone.

This environment hurt the hospital in several ways. It hurt patient-care relationships in a department where every move could prove critical. Residents tried to hide their lack of knowledge from others for fear of being eliminated. They worked themselves into exhaustion, sacrificing their own health, hurting relationships outside the workplace, and further endangering their patients' care. And nobody was having fun.

To change this negative situation, the director proposed two new ideas. First, he asked to admit six residents and keep them—no eliminations. Then he asked the staff to focus more energy on simply having fun. The staff laughed long and hard at the two suggestions but agreed to try the plan for one year.

A cultural shift began at once. At first, in their attempts to have fun, the staff members just had more parties and social functions. But these imposed activities soon gave way to spontaneous enjoyment of each other's company. The residents, no longer fearing the loss of their position, began asking more questions, admitting their mistakes, and actually learning from the nurses and more experienced staff. The quality of care and education increased dramatically.

What's more, the new environment began to draw out unhealthy personal habits the residents and other staff had been hiding. Their attempts at fun soon revealed that tired, exhausted people can not enjoy such activities. "Herein lay the radical change. By altering the surgery schedule and adding exercise and nutrition programs for the staff, the doctors began to experience their professional lives as congruent with their missions as healers. For some of them, this change also facilitated their confronting their own workaholism."[7]

At the end of the experiment, the staff pronounced the new changes a resounding success. In addition to expressing an increased satisfaction with their jobs, they got to know each other personally, laughed more, and became more productive and interdependent.

Two Kinds of Organizations

The character ladder leads to a relational organization—a community—that honors the completion of tasks. The capacity ladder typically leads to a task-driven organization, at the expense of people. This ladder creates people-users—leaders who use followers for their own benefit, to further their own success. But leaders on the character ladder treat *people* as the object and focus of their success. They lead for the benefit of their people, not just their own benefit.

Capacity-ladder-only organizations strive for accountability in order to get things done, but they do so at the expense of people's hearts. When leaders lose the hearts of their people, their peoples' productivity will suffer. Creativity will wane. Initiative will die. Achieving a vision requires a unity of hand and heart, of vocation and soul. To break through the ceiling on productivity, people must understand that what they do synchronizes with who they are. When the culture of an organization honors the achievement of a goal over the health of its people, leaders and followers will learn to hide their hearts in an attempt to reach that goal, even at the expense of their vision, their own souls, and, ultimately, the soul of the organization.

On the character ladder, the depth of influence is honored above the height of position. Living the truth is more important than living for success. Instead of making hasty moves that may harm relational investments, character-ladder leaders will protect relationships, even though commitment, patience, and time can be costly. Mistakes and failures are viewed through the farsighted lens of personal and organizational development, rather than through the nearsighted lens of short-term results. Leaders in relational organizations affirm the wisdom of Winston Churchill when he said, "Success is going from failure to failure with great enthusiasm."[8] Trust develops in such places, and people learn things about each other they never knew before, finding deeper strengths that can sometimes remain hidden behind roles.

Many employees, group members, and even family members share a common frustration: they don't like being pigeonholed in a specific role, vocation, or stereotype. Yet leaders will find it difficult to overcome faulty assumptions unless they make the commitment to look beyond a person's current job status, gender, race, or other potential speck in the leader's eye. The next time you wish *If only I had a person who could . . .* , stop to consider that maybe the person already exists in your organization but may not feel safe enough to reveal his or her strengths.

The Big Five accounting firm Deloitte & Touche learned this lesson the hard way. After making what they thought were significant efforts to recruit and retain talented women in their firm, they discovered ten years later that they were actually driving women away. They did a study to find out why and discovered what their CEO, Mike Cook, called unintentional discrimination and unwitting paternalism. It seems that when career-advancing assignments came up, usually requiring travel and time away from home, the partners assumed that the women would not want to be away from home. So the women never got the chance to prove themselves, as the male partners tried to "protect" them from travel. And when company outings were planned, senior partners never stopped to consider that fishing trips and golfing might exclude the women from meaningful interaction. Since the study, Deloitte & Touche has taken bold steps to counter the subtle discrimination, including assigning mentors to younger women to discover their talents and real aspirations.[9]

When it comes right down to it, it's not what we do that brings fulfillment, but with whom we do those things. Fulfillment sprouts from how well we connect with those around us every day as we pursue our careers, raise our families, or volunteer our time. Like a plant with a good root system in the right soil, these connections produce tremendous fruit. What kinds of fruit?

Experiencing Acceptance

One fruit of interdependent relationships of grace is that people experience unconditional acceptance. Experiencing and offering acceptance is far from merely practicing some technique; rather, acceptance arises from a process requiring frequent, interactive communication in committed relationships. Commitment is very important to the experience of acceptance. Acceptance only lasts as long as the commitment lasts, because commitment creates a soul connection that takes relationships beyond their utilitarian functions.

To experience acceptance, we must first *admit our need* for acceptance from others. Then we must take the next step and *receive* expressions of acceptance from others. Accepting acceptance empowers us to confer acceptance. This is why we wrote this book for the nine out of ten who say they believe in God, because the source of unconditional acceptance traces back to God. If we cannot receive acceptance, we cannot confer it on others. Thousands struggle with accepting others, not realizing that the answer lies in first accepting acceptance.

Experiencing acceptance is a winding, two-way street, sometimes full of potholes from past stormy relationships and roadblocks thrown up by our own independent spirits. Yet the interactive process of giving and receiving acceptance enables you to value who others are, rather than just what they can do. And people learn to accept you for who you are, rather than placing false expectations on you, or valuing you for what you can provide them.

If people affirm us for who we are, this ignites a desire to please them. If we love and are loved in spite of what we know about others or what they know about us, we become empowered to change for the better. The same proves true in our relationship with God. If we know God loves us, in spite of who we are, this ignites a desire to please God. But if we lack a sense of acceptance, either from God or from others, we become edgy and apprehensive, and we second-guess others.

Practicing acceptance does not mean we abandon performance standards or accountability in our organizations. In healthy organizations, accountability must be established as the norm. It's the only effective way of measuring performance and viability. An organization without accountability is a ship without a rudder. But to maintain a basis for healthy accountability, the organization must also accept its role as a community.

Expressing acceptance to others will never lower performance. In fact, it does just the opposite. We have watched teams in our workshops transformed by beginning the process of offering acceptance to each other. The tool we use is actually quite simple, providing a way to express basic affirmations to each other. Yet the process of actually doing the affirmation tool is profound. (See Figure 4.2.) Formerly stoic men and women have wept openly upon hearing, sometimes for the first time, how much their team members appreciate what they do and who they are. On an interesting note, the affirmation doesn't have to come from the boss to have a profound effect. In fact, sometimes it's the boss who needs the affirmation the most, even though bosses may think they need it least. We all need affirmation and acceptance to reach our true potential.

Georgia had been laid off from her previous position as a bookkeeper. Her previous managers had criticized her work, constantly pointing out her errors and convincing her that she was not capable of anything more. So when she found a different job as a receptionist, she considered herself lucky.

In her new work environment, her peers and boss affirmed her conscientiousness; attention to detail; and sensitive, caring heart. At first, she had difficulty believing them. After a few months of this treatment, she took a risk and mentioned her bookkeeping experience. Soon her boss began giving her small accounting tasks to test her abilities. Though she obsessed a bit, for fear of making any mistakes, it became clear that she not only was good at this but enjoyed it a great deal more than answering phones. More affirmation from her boss and peers ensued. Her speed and accuracy improved. Soon other parts of the organization began to notice her abilities and wondered if they could share in this newfound treasure. Georgia now does excellent bookkeeping and accounting work for four different departments.

Ron Willingham, whose organization, Integrity Systems, has trained over a million sales professionals to be more productive,

Figure 4.2. The Affirmation Tool

accepting
adaptable
administrator
adventurous
affirming
analytical
artist
assertive
authentic
authoritative
benevolent
bold
called
can-do
careful
change agent
charismatic
comforting
committed
communicative
compassionate
concerned
connected
conscientious
controlled
creative
credible
cunning
decisive
deliberate
dependable
destined
detail-oriented
determined
discerning
disciplined
doctrinally sound
encouraging
energetic
enterprising
even-keeled
exciting
exemplary
experienced
factual
faithful
festive
firm
flexible
focused
fun-loving
future-thinking
generous

gentle
genuine
gifted
giving
goal-driven
good
gracious
gregarious
group-oriented
healer
helpful
honest
honorable
humble
humorous
imaginative
industrious
influential
ingenious
initiator
inquisitive
insightful
intelligent
in-touch
joyful
kind
knowledgeable
leading
listening heart
loving
loyal
mature
meek
mentor
merciful
motivated
motivator
nurturing
observant
optimistic
orderly
organized
original
passionate
pastor
patient
peacemaker
persistent
persuasive
pioneering
point-person
polished
positive

powerful
practical
precise
predictable
principled
promoting
prophetic
protector
purposeful
real
relational
relevant
respectful
risk taker
sacrificial
scheduled
scholastic
secure
self-controlled
selfless
sensitive

service-oriented
shepherd
shrewd
spiritual
spontaneous
stable
strong
successful
sympathetic
taking charge
talented
thoughtful
tolerant
trusted
very verbal
visionary
vulnerable
watchful
wealthy
winsome
wise

I feel most strongly that this person is:

1. _____

2. _____

3. _____

4. _____

5. _____

6. _____

7. _____

8. _____

9. _____

10. _____

Notes:

recognizes our need for acceptance to be and do our best: "In our courses, we train facilitators to create a noncritical atmosphere and give unconditional acceptance to people. To look at them and see God-valued people. To listen without biases. To listen nonjudgmentally. To look for and focus on their strengths. Many people fight us at first, feeling uncomfortable at receiving unconditional acceptance—not being accustomed to it. Many have suffered abuse, confusion and rejection to the point that unconsciously they aren't comfortable with real acceptance."[10]

Uncomfortable or not, experiencing acceptance in relationships of grace, in an environment of grace, has far-reaching benefits. For instance, one of the fundamental reasons for the resounding success of most twelve-step recovery programs stems from their commitment to creating a group of people who in dependence on God learn of each other's shortcomings and keep coming back. Such commitment creates the dynamic of unconditional acceptance that participants need in order for them to face the truth objectively and to begin the climb to a healthier life. Gracious connections like these can be experienced in ordinary relationships, too, not just in twelve-step programs or in therapeutic sessions with professionals.

Some assume that extending such grace will lead to abuses—that people will take advantage of us and our organizations. But sincere acceptance, motivated by heartfelt concern rather than manipulation, rarely produces such results. Still, the possibility does exist, but the risks are worth the occasional need to reprimand and confront such abusers. In fact, when we confront those who abuse grace, the power of acceptance becomes even more evident.

Robert Greenleaf, the father of the modern servant-leadership movement, learned grace this way. While a student at Carleton College, Greenleaf began a lifelong friendship with the college president, Donald Cowling. They might never have met had Greenleaf "not been a student who occasionally got into trouble and found [him]self in his office with some explaining to do."

During those office visits, Greenleaf discovered a man "with deep and dependable understanding and compassion and with an unequivocal belief in freedom for the human spirit to flower." In the process of being confronted with his failures, Greenleaf experienced deep acceptance. In his writings, he laments those who never have such an opportunity: "I am sorry for those who have never gotten into trouble because they really cannot share my experience. It is one thing to experience compassion intellectually, or even to give it. It is quite another thing to receive compassion when one knows that all one is entitled to is justice."[11]

Telling the Truth

Another fruit of relationships of grace is honesty. When people experience grace despite their failures, they gain the strength to face the truth without fear. Those who live amid ungracious relationships learn to hide the truth. This is why capacity-ladder leaders tend to focus on the *appearance* of performance rather than on authentic performance. In such situations, other people can easily become scapegoats when things go wrong. Mistakes get concealed. Blame abounds. The rules change expeditiously, sometimes in a frantic effort to cover the leader's backside. This kind of behavior signals imminent danger for any company, organization, family, and perhaps even individuals themselves.

Charlotte Roberts, an author and specialist in executive team issues, recalls an example of suppressing the truth that occurred during a meeting at a small glass-bottle manufacturing company. In setting the ground rules for the meeting, the manager of quality control suggested that they all be "honest" with each other. But the production manager replied with a smirk, "I can only be flexibly honest. For instance, if I can sneak bottles past quality control to make my production bonus, I will." Within seconds, the quality control manager had to be physically restrained in order to prevent a brawl. For you see, his bonus suffered as the quality of the bottles fell.[12] The managers had no relational context in which to deal with the real issues honestly.

Though perhaps not evident on the surface, people and organizations usually end up hurt and anemic because of such internal bleeding. Kouzes and Posner write, "The best leaders want to get closer to others, want to be more intimate with others, than do the poorer performers," and, "All the evidence points in the same direction . . . the quality of our relationships has a protective effect. . . . You can have the best job in the world and make more money than Bill Gates, but if you lack close social ties you may not live to enjoy it."[13] Not only do relationships of grace improve productivity and nurture our hearts, but they improve our physical health as well. Think of the impact all this could have on the productivity and well-being of your business, organization, or family.

Fruit Within Our Reach

Like acceptance, affirmation, and honesty, the fruits of relationships of grace can seem like ripe, red delicious apples hanging just beyond your yearning grasp. You know they would taste good and nourish you, but you may wonder, *What good is fruit if it cannot be reached?* Years of counterproductive relational and environmental practices may leave some leaders skeptical. But these words about the fruit of gracious community are not intended as a tease to your hungry soul. The wonderful thing is, relationships of grace can form rather quickly.

For instance, a couple from Mexico came to our workshop in Phoenix. Just a year later they showed up again, excited to repeat the workshop in Los Angeles. When Bruce asked them why, they invited him to have lunch with some friends they had brought along. During the meal, a medical doctor, a school principal, and others shared significant changes and fruit that had been borne in their marriages, families, and careers. All this and more came from the influence of that one couple, who upon returning to Mexico a few months earlier, shared some of what they had learned about living and working in relationships of grace.

When our needs are met amid relationships of grace, we become fulfilled. In fulfillment, we give back to the community in measure far greater than we could as isolated individuals. When we understand and admit how much we need each other, we can leave behind our overdependence on lonely capacity ladders and begin forming the basis for caring communities where ordinary people accomplish extraordinary things, including the development of their character.

Along with becoming fulfilled and experiencing greater productivity, we may actually enjoy work more. When we love others and are loved by others in our workplace, we will do better work. People who live in this kind of sustaining community have far more fun as they enjoy each other's personalities and spirits. These are just a few of the fruits awaiting those who choose to foster and live in community. We'll discover more as we ascend the rungs of the character ladder.

Choosing Wisely

Only the character ladder promotes such a sustaining community. It's longer, so it takes more time to climb. It's stronger, so it is able to support more weight at greater heights. It's also more expensive and harder to manufacture.

On the character ladder, relationships of grace—committed relationships that meet needs—support each rung in tandem with an environment of grace. Every step in the chapters that follow will show just how important purposeful, intimate human interactions are in developing and sustaining leaders' character and influence. Relationships provide the context for the affirmation and application of the principles embedded in the rungs.

We believe thousands of leaders have become disillusioned with the capacity ladder. It is incomplete. It is lonely. It doesn't satisfy. We also believe that perhaps millions of emerging leaders are seeking a different kind of ladder. Many leaders are ready to receive power instead of pursuing it at the expense of their hearts. They yearn to experience community instead of standing alone at the top of a pyramid. They long to create environments that inspire the soul.

Are you ready to learn how? If so, you are about to embark on a climb of profound and enduring consequences, a climb that takes you above and beyond *your* best to find *God's* best. Having learned about the rails of environment and relationships, we must now test the rungs.

Grabbing Hold

- How much of what you do is truly a reflection of who you are? Why?
- Which ladder best describes the environment and relationships of your life right now?
- Because fulfillment requires that we receive acceptance, affirmation, and other expressions of love, why do some people work exclusively for wealth, position, and status?
- What needs do you think you have?

Chapter Five

The First Rung

Stepping Up Through an Act of Trust

> It is a dangerous business to arrive in eternity with
> possibilities which one himself has prevented from
> becoming actualities. Possibility is a hint from God.
> A person must follow it . . . if God does not want it,
> then let him hinder it; the person must not hinder
> it himself.
> —*Søren Kierkegaard*

Five years into marriage, Bill's wife, Grace, chose a creative way to get his attention. One evening when he got home from work, Grace greeted him at the door with a blunt directive: "We need to go for a ride," she said.

Her strained tone and piercing eyes told Bill she had something important in mind. Very astutely he reasoned, "I'm in trouble," and tried to stall by asking, "What about the kids?"

"I took care of them," Grace replied. "They'll be fine."

Heading for the door to their old Chrysler, Bill worried, "What did I do? What did she find out?" By the time he had settled behind the steering wheel, he had compiled his initial list of defenses and alibis. "Where to?" he asked with cucumber-like coolness and cheer.

"Drive north," she said.

They drove for what seemed the longest thirty minutes of Bill's life. He didn't say a word, and neither did Grace, until she instructed Bill to pull over into an almost empty parking lot. Although his sweat had now soaked through his suit, he wasn't about to let her see his nervousness, so he kept quiet. Grace had never done anything even remotely like this before. This was her call.

Bill could see she had prepared well for this moment. Her peace and clear presence of mind further unnerved him. After a long pause, Grace finally spoke.

"I want you to know that you are a great father, a good provider, and I know that you love me, but I am extremely unhappy, and—"

"What? How dare you!" Bill interrupted. "Yes, I am a good father. I work hard for my family. How can you say you're not happy?" He thought: "This isn't about me. It's about her. She's got a problem."

Continuing to vent his angry response, Bill blurted out other personal accolades to elicit remorse from her. But they didn't work. So he got out of the car and stormed around, playing the wounded spouse role to the hilt. "How dare she!" Bill grumbled to himself. When he finally got back into the car, Grace was still calm and peaceful, completely unmoved by his antics. Then, very simply, she asked, "Don't you want to know *why* I am so unhappy?"

"Well . . . uh . . . yes," Bill responded. "Why?"

"You will not let me love you," she replied. Then, after a brief pause, "You do not even try to trust me. I love you. I want to be all I can for you, but you won't let me. Please hear me."

Tears filled her eyes. "This is so serious," Grace continued. "You cannot just love me. To have a relationship, I have to be able to love you!" She explained how Bill's inability to trust was slowly decaying their marriage, his relationship with his kids, and his influence.

For five years Bill had kept his life hidden from Grace. He tested her love in many ways, not willing to believe it could be trusted. He felt she would not be able to handle the real Bill. Each rejection of her sincere, loving attempts to win his heart had caused Grace tremendous pain. Yet, in the face of it all, instead of using condemnation or put-downs, she responded with strength and deep commitment, giving Bill the courage to open his life for review by someone who loved him deeply. According to Bill, "For the first time, I chose to trust Grace with me."

Beginning the Climb

This is where we begin our climb up the character ladder: with an act of trust. We all entrust ourselves to something, whether it's God, money, our spouse, our career, our productivity, ourselves, or whatever. Our character, and therefore our influence, flows from our choices of whom, what, when, and where we believe. Such trust— often referred to as faith—lives at the center of our lives, shaping who we are. The impetus to make a step of faith begins in the heart—the inner part of us that longs to be known but is never fully knowable by anyone but the Creator.

With each interpersonal interaction, a struggle of trust ensues. The struggle pushes and pulls at our heartstrings. We groan inwardly, wishing for a soul mate who truly understands us: Don't you see my potential? Can't you see the real me longing to get out? Won't you trust me?

Yet we also groan at the thought of being completely known: What would people think if they knew the truth about me? Would their friendship and love endure if they knew how I sometimes act and feel? Should they trust me?

Bill asked himself those same questions a thousand times. With Grace, they all boiled down to one question that evening: "Could trusting my wife with who I am help fix my heart?"

Choices of the Heart

The heart—the inner life, shaped primarily by trust—molds our motives. Our motives establish our values. And our values govern our actions. What we believe about ourselves takes root and is nourished in our hearts. And it's from the heart that our destiny— our ultimate influence and value—flows.

No matter how secret we think they are, we expose our heart beliefs through the choices we make. If we have faith in a bridge, we will trust it enough to choose to drive over it. If we have faith in our spouse, we will choose to reveal ourselves to him or her. If we trust in God, our faith will enable us to escape being molded by circumstances or seduced by opportunities as we strive to make the best choices.

At times, trust comes easily. There are also moments when choosing to trust can seem a life-threatening leap into the unknown, or at least an unsteady step in a suspicious direction. We may be tempted to conclude that when choosing trust seems most questionable or difficult, trust will dissolve more easily. Perhaps in some cases this is true. But strangely, the opposite is often true. Spouses have been known to defend their partner's faithfulness, even when the evidence to the contrary is overwhelming. Employees or students may overlook the obvious faults of an employer or teacher, even putting themselves in great danger. Such was the case with one former senior advisor to the President of the United States.

In his book, *All Too Human*, George Stephanopoulos recalls learning as an altar boy how just doing his job, no matter how insignificant it seemed, could accomplish significant things under the right circumstances. He took this belief with him into the campaign for the presidency where he learned that "doing good" meant defending Bill Clinton from seemingly endless allegations of wrongdoing.

Stephanopoulos had heard the rumors about Clinton's personal problems, but was willing to put them in the past for the sake of his own ambitious dreams, ideals, and desire to accomplish a greater good for the people of the United States. After watching Clinton campaign, he soon became convinced that this man could help turn his dreams into reality. In effect, he became a Clinton groupie—a "true believer"—even, as later events unfolded, against his own gut instincts.

Stephanopoulos vehemently and effectively defended Clinton against charges of draft dodging until John King of the Associated Press stunned him with a copy of Clinton's draft notice. Did Stephanopoulos begin to doubt the president? Did he feel like a dupe? Of course he did. But instead of turning tail and running, he chose to defy the inherent danger of trusting someone who proved untrustworthy. Each time a betrayal occurred he searched for a reason to stay. And he always seemed to find one. So did the American people, who elected Bill Clinton twice, in spite of the scandals.

Stephanopoulos's autobiographical musings give us some insight into why we choose to put our faith in dishonest leaders. Stephanopoulos set aside his doubts about Clinton for the sake of their common goals, his own ambition, and his determination to not let the attackers win. More than love, it may have been personal pride that kept him in the fight for the Clintons, because if Clinton looked bad, Stephanopoulos looked bad and so did their party and their agenda. In other words, Stephanopoulos believed that the end sometimes justifies the means—that just doing your job, no matter what, under the right circumstances, may get you where you want to go.

Choosing whom to trust is never as simple as it may appear on the surface. George Stephanopoulos eventually did quit, deciding he could not endure the stress of another term. Though Stephanopoulos decided his own integrity was at risk by staying, many others stuck by the President's side, feeling just as convinced of their justifications. Even after the Monica Lewinsky story broke, Stephanopoulos admitted that he wasn't sure how he would have handled the affair if he was still by Clinton's side:

"The truth is I couldn't really know what I would do because I wasn't there—in the Oval, inhaling that high-octane White House air, sitting in my usual chair, resting my forearm on his broad oak desk as the president of the United States looked me in the eye and put his hand on mine and begged me to believe him just one more time."

No matter what you think of Clinton or Stephanopoulos, this account illustrates just how difficult trust is to nail down. It also illustrates that when the hammer falls, the reasons for our trust don't rest solely on the character of those we choose to follow. Our reasons for trusting can usually be found deep within our own character as well.

Risky Business

The possibility of betrayal makes trust a risky business. And the risks aren't limited to the sphere of human interaction. Like the friends of the biblical figure Job, many of us question God, particularly when bad things happen to reasonably good people. The risk in trust presents a significant quandary in our quest to climb the character ladder, because the first rung is all about trust. First we must trust God and, in turn, trust others. As Figure 5.1 illustrates, the first rung is *trust God and others with me*. But what motivates us to take this initial step?

Foster Friess, one of the world's leading investment advisers, once faced this challenge. Raised by a rugged individualist father, who was raised by a frontiersman grandfather, Friess learned the values of willpower and determination against all odds. Believing that if he worked hard he could do anything, he became high school class president and captain of the basketball team, the golf team, and the track team: "All those things," Friess says, "that are possible when you only have ten kids in your class."

He went on to prove himself at the University of Wisconsin, becoming president of his fraternity and graduating as one of the top ten most outstanding seniors. During the late 1970s, he earned a six-figure income through an innovative sales philosophy that said, "There are only two reasons I won't get that client by the end of the year—either they'll die or I'll die."

Finally, Friess reached what he thought was the pinnacle of success. He had nice cars, a nice house on a two-acre lot in the best part of town, a beautiful wife, and kids in private school. He thought he had it all, but he didn't.

"It was as if I had my ladder up against a wall and as I went rung after rung after rung and got to the top rung, I looked at the roof, and there was nothing but pigeons up there. There was a hollowness. There was a boredom."

His marriage was suffering. He and his wife went through five counselors, to no avail. He couldn't get along with his kids. About

Figure 5.1. The First Rung of the Character Ladder

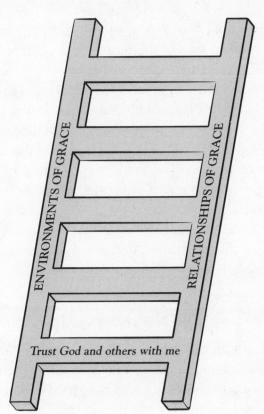

this time, Friess's fourth son, Michael, developed a high fever that wouldn't go down. They rushed him to the hospital around midnight and soon received the diagnosis. Michael had contracted spinal meningitis. The doctors handed Friess and his wife a paper bag with Michael's small pajamas, telling Friess to burn it to protect their other children from infection.

Walking into his son's hospital room in the wee hours of the morning, Friess looked through the cold steel bed rails into the fever-clouded eyes of his son. Helplessly he watched as those normally bright blue eyes hazed over and then slowly rolled back, revealing nothing but the whites. That was the moment when "[f]or Foster Friess the myth of self-sufficiency was burst."[2]

In order to take this step, we must allow the myth of self-sufficiency to end. In a sense, this means we must let our seed of destiny fall to the ground and be buried, because this is the only way it can begin to germinate and grow.[3] We must awaken to our need for God and each other. Whatever hinders our character, whatever fulfillment we lack, whatever prevents us from reaching our destiny—these things awaken us to our needs. Needs like these can be met only by placing trust in God and others. We may be tempted to deny these needs or to try to meet them through the pursuit of rights or power. But it is our need for God's care and commitment, our need for others' care and commitment, that motivates us to take the first step in climbing the character ladder. Without an awareness of our needs, the step is impossible to take.

The Nature of God

When we reflect on the nature of our Creator, we gain a sense of these deeper needs of our heart. The degree to which we entrust ourselves to the Supreme Being demonstrates the level at which we have understood the character of that Being. Each of us must ask, Is God good or capricious? Is my Creator personal and intimately aware of my life, or just some impersonal force that sets things spinning in motion like a gigantic clock? Is the Almighty committed to protecting me, or prone to abandoning me when troubles come? If we trust that God is good by nature, we will honor God's authority and power in our lives.

Maybe it's easiest to explain the impact of understanding God's nature and authority by comparing the first steps of the capacity and character ladders. At the bottom of the capacity ladder, we focus on discovering what *we* can do, whereas on the character ladder, we focus on discovering what *God* can do. Early on the capacity ladder, we awaken to our potential *for* God—what we think we can offer to God and this world. On the character ladder, we awaken to our destiny *under* God.

In a sense, on the first step of the capacity ladder, I begin to let me be me, seeking my own unique way in the world, whereas on the first step of the character ladder, I choose to let God be God, understanding that God's ways are not mine. Of course, this analogy does not hold up after we've spent a lot of time on the character ladder, because when I use its rungs consistently, my way ever more closely resembles God's way—everything I *do* begins to reflect who I was created to *be*. This merging between our plans and God's intentions for our character is the goal of the character ladder.

Just as proper understanding of the Creator's nature and authority can encourage trust, improper understanding can hinder our trust. Some people assume that learning about God's bigness necessitates negative obsession with their own smallness. You might hear them say things like "I am not valuable" or "I have nothing to offer." Such statements do not honor the nature and authority of God; they demean it. After all, the Creator called creation good, including humans. Such negative self-statements only reveal a genuine lack of ability, a poor self-image, or a false spirituality.

One day a rabbi, in a frenzy of religious passion, rushed in before the ark, fell to his knees, and started beating his breast, crying, "I'm nobody! I'm nobody!"

The cantor of the synagogue, impressed by this display, joined the rabbi on his knees, saying, "I'm nobody! I'm nobody!"

The custodian watching from the corner, couldn't restrain himself either. He joined the other two on his knees, calling out, "I'm nobody! I'm nobody!"

At which point the rabbi, nudging the cantor with his elbow, pointed at the custodian and said, "Look who thinks he's nobody!"[4]

God has no desire for us to belittle ourselves in a false humility. Instead, our acknowledging God's nature creates genuine humility. When we come face-to-face with the strength of God—not as worthless people but as people who are willing to present all our strengths, talents, and influence to the strong hands of a loving Creator—we demonstrate our trust in God's nature and authority. Sure, we bring our needs and weaknesses too, but trusting God with who we are has nothing to do with demeaning our personal value.

Trusting God has to do with accepting who God is and accepting who we are in the context of God's plan. It has to do with receiving the protection we need to trust others. Entrusting ourselves to God is the essence of the biblical understanding of humility.

Humble Beginnings

A verse in the Bible says, "Humble yourselves, therefore, under God's mighty hand, that he may lift you up in due time."[5] People who let God be God and entrust their lives to their Creator understand who has the ultimate responsibility for determining their value and destiny. God does.

Leaving our value and destiny in God's hands can be disconcerting for those who have not come to terms with the biblical reality of a loving, personal God. Disconcerting or not, don't miss this point: unless we trust God with our potential, we will be robbed of God's plan for our destiny. When God asks us to let our seed of destiny be buried in the soil of relationships, it is because humility—recognizing that God is God and we are not—is the only catalyst that can enable our character to germinate properly. Why is humility so important?

It's those vertical rails. God's plan for our destiny involves meaningful interaction with other human beings in communities and environments of grace. We must interact with others who, like us, need grace. People who have their own agendas, weaknesses, sins, and flawed motives. People with care, strengths, love, and inspiring vision. All human beings come into our lives with a mixed bag of strengths and weaknesses—traits that engender trust and attributes that give us good reason to write these people off. Yet people are part of God's plan for preparing us for our legacy. God created us for community. God created us to trust him and to trust others with the deepest parts of our lives. This trust requires humility.

In one sense, we could say that such humility and trust are in short supply these days. We seem to have an epidemic of pride and

mistrust in our communities. Interpersonal and intercultural feelings ranging from complacent indifference to abject fear expose our
mistrust toward other people and other cultures. In another sense,
we routinely humble ourselves and trust others on a daily basis
whenever we depend on them for things we cannot supply ourselves. As Robert Shaw writes in *Trust in the Balance,* "We cannot
survive without others. Thus, we trust because we have no choice
but to depend on other people. How many of us can produce our
own food and water? Cure ourselves when we are sick? Build a protective shelter? In each case, we must rely on the good will and ability of others if we are to survive."[6] We will never be able to trust
everyone, but we cannot live a fulfilled life without trusting lots of
people.

In a community and environment of grace, we are able to take
steps of trust with people very different from ourselves, in some
cases even misfits or moguls we may have previously avoided. If
you've never seen this in action, you may want to drop in on a local
Alcoholics Anonymous meeting sometime. Most likely you'll find
politicians and paupers, Anglos and African Americans, men and
women, young and old, all sharing in each other's process of bat-
tling addiction. If humility and trust, expressed in statements like,
"Hi, I'm Rick, and I'm an alcoholic," can begin to break the grip of
alcoholism, imagine what trust can do to achieve "hard" business
results, or to heal your marriage or family.

Receiving the care and concern of others who are different
from ourselves can be messy and sometimes chaotic. As Philip
Yancey warns in *Church: Why Bother?* "A downtown church that
does not turn away the poor, the homeless, or the unpredictable
risks attracting people who may disrupt the worship service." But
when we refuse to turn away people different from ourselves, accepting them for who they are, we will be amazed at how little we
have sacrificed and how much we have gained. To paraphrase the
apostle Paul, the poor, the foolish, and the weak of this world will
astonish the rich, the wise, and the strong.[7] Trust should not be re-
served for a small group of people who look, think, and act in ways

very similar to ourselves. Such a cliquish approach serves to extend our own egos rather than challenge us to grow. Margaret Wheatley and Myron Kellner-Rogers of the Berkana Institute caution us about this trend toward uniformity in their analysis of so-called virtual communities: "The great potential of a world connected electronically is being used in part to create stronger boundaries that keep us isolated from one another. Through the Web, we can seek relationships with others who are exactly like us. We are responding to our instinct of community, but we form highly specialized groups in our own image, groups that reinforce our separateness from the rest of society. We are not asked to contribute our uniqueness, only our sameness. We are not asked to encounter, much less celebrate, the fact that we need one another's gifts.[8]

Choosing to trust people, especially those who are different from ourselves, has a lot to do with trusting the One who is managing the path of our lives. When we understand and trust that our destiny rests in God's hands, we can with greater patience endure negative circumstances and difficult relationships. More important, as was the case with Bill and Grace in the story that began this chapter, we gain the strength we need to trust people who have our best interests at heart, even at the risk of pain or personal loss. Why? Because we believe that God will work it out, somehow, for our good, no matter what happens.[9]

Genuine Humility

When we entrust ourselves to God in this way, humility creates increasing gratitude and decreasing greed. Those who learn to trust God have less and less desire to possess somebody else's stuff in order to be content. They don't feel compelled to ask the question comedian Rita Rudner does in her book, *Naked Beneath My Clothes*: "If I can't have it all, can I at least have some of yours?"[10] Further, those who let God be God recognize that all they have, no matter how much or how little, comes as a gift. So they become increasingly thankful for all they have.

Whenever we encounter greed, lust, or avarice in a person, we can be sure that lack of trust in God is at the root. Lack of trust also produces lack of gratitude. Perhaps this is why God began the Ten Commandments with "I am the Lord your God . . . you shall have no other gods before me," and concluded with, "You shall not covet . . . anything that belongs to your neighbor."[11] Entrusting ourselves to God—genuine humility—leads to a thankful, contented heart. One presupposes the other.

Of course, finding such genuine humility in anyone 100 percent of the time represents a tall order for about 100 percent of humanity. Therefore, as George Stephanopoulos demonstrated, choosing whom to trust can be a messy business.

We can't trust just anyone with our innermost being, even if he or she asks us to. This would be foolish and possibly do more harm than good. But we must trust someone, so it becomes a question of whom.

Thankfully, God's design for our destiny primarily calls for common, easy-to-find materials—the stuff of everyday life and everyday people and everyday struggles. It's from such raw materials that God fashions the finest leaders—the ones who leave an enduring legacy—the ones who give us the strength to move forward into our destiny.

Do you want to leave a lasting legacy—one that will benefit generations to come? Do you want to live for a greater purpose—the kind that will sustain you amid contrary circumstance? Do you long to live in relationships of trust where you are fully known and know others more fully? Do you hope for the day when what you do matches who you are? If so, take the first step up the character ladder. "Men of genius are admired. Men of wealth are envied. Men of power are feared," Arthur Friedman once said, "but only men of character are trusted."[12]

With eyes wide open, take a step of faith, expressing your willingness to trust God and others with *you*. Don't prevent the possibilities that God has placed before you from becoming a reality. Trust the protection of the Almighty to guard and keep you. God is big enough to keep you safe as you choose to entrust yourself to those who can be trusted. Step up. Then prepare for the next rung.

Grabbing Hold

- Who trusts you?
- How do your actions substantiate the value you place on humility?
- What does hiding what is true about you cost you? What does it cost others?

Chapter Six

The Second Rung

Choosing Vulnerability

One of the reasons our society has become such a
mess is that we're isolated from each other.
—*Maggie Kuhn*

Bruce remembers the fear of being alone. Really alone. Lost in a
dark forest, separated from his group, he felt terribly isolated and
didn't know what to do about it. Terror gripped his eight-year-old
heart.

Many adults—especially leaders—wander into dark forests of
isolation. They don't live alone, but they live apart from the benefit of significant others speaking into their lives. Some leaders feel
more comfortable with isolation than they do with letting people
get close to them. They depend on personal distance for protection.
We may sense something wrong as we watch such leaders deal with
the pressures, expectations, and commitments of success and expanding influence. But like Bruce in the forest, most leaders don't
know what to do about their isolation.

The Dark Wood

Lonely leaders are everywhere, although power or wealth may anes-
thetize their souls and soothe them into a false sense of security.
Many leaders suddenly wake up to find themselves like the character in Dante's *Divine Comedy:* "In the middle of the road of my life
I awoke in a dark wood where the true way was wholly lost."

Although they are surrounded by people, these leaders can't seem to connect in meaningful ways. They suffer from their self-imposed separation, and so do those they influence.

A number of years ago, in graduate school, Bruce fashioned a project around one particular leadership dysfunction: deception. The title reflected his jaundiced perception of some leaders. He called it "Everybody Lies, But Leaders Do It Better." He interviewed leaders who had deceived and been publicly caught, from the fields of medicine, journalism, law and law enforcement, the church, and so forth. (He gave the politicians a break on this one and left them alone.) A number of these leaders were making wonderful recoveries.

The interviews exposed isolation as the primary reason the leaders gave themselves permission to lie. Their isolation was not a spatial separation—people were constantly around these leaders—but a soul separation from others. And it wasn't like the God-appointed isolation God gave Moses in the desert, but rather a state of being lost in Dante's dark wood. Often, the further up leaders are on the capacity ladder or the longer they've occupied the top rung, the worse the problem gets. Isolation factors heavily not only in deception but in many other relational difficulties as well.

Isolation robs leaders of reaching God's intended destiny. In an interview, Howard Hendricks, the founder of a respected leadership center in Dallas, said on this subject, "When I meet with leaders, I simply assume society has infected them and they have not lived in authentic communities and that this reality will eventually hurt them." We would add to his statement, "and hurt those who follow them."

Getting Out of the Woods

How do we overcome the isolation that threatens to rob us of our influence? The answer is found in the second rung on the character ladder—*choose vulnerability*. (See Figure 6.1.) But what is vulnerability? And how does it work?

Figure 6.1. The Second Rung of the Character Ladder

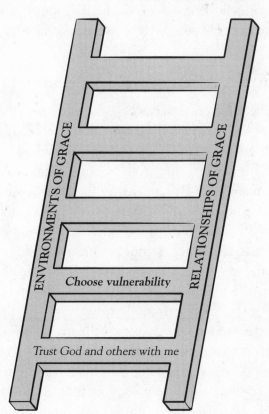

To be vulnerable means to come under another's influence. Some time ago, a widely respected business leader taught Bruce several helpful skills in dealing with people. However, as Bruce grew to know this man, he began to resist his influence. It wasn't an intentional resistance, just an instinctive hesitation. The reason?

Intuitively, Bruce understood that by giving this man authority, he would be giving him influence in Bruce's life. Why? Because authority is designed to influence, to guide in making major choices, and to shape destiny. Yet this man was the kind of leader who would not submit his own needs or issues to the counsel of others. He shared much about his life but was not knowable or teachable in critical areas, areas in which Bruce and others observed he needed to grow. Automatically, Bruce biased himself against this man's teaching and mentoring. He decided he could not completely trust him.

A Historical Example of a Vulnerable Leader

William Wilberforce once faced this issue of vulnerability. As a personal friend of William Pitt, the soon-to-be prime minister of Great Britain, Wilberforce's early political career looked rather bright, even though his personal life and character seemed a bit wanting. As a popular member of Parliament, Wilberforce relished his power and prestige and especially the parties around London, which he frequented with gusto. But through the encouragement of an old college friend, Isaac Milner, a tutor at Queen's College Cambridge, Wilberforce began to take a serious look at his life, leading to an encounter with the claims of Jesus. After much personal struggle, Wilberforce trusted God with his destiny, thus beginning his ascent up the character ladder. He considered the implications of his decision to trust God, soon concluding through personal study that he should leave politics and become a minister. Thankfully, Wilberforce's personal study also convinced him that he must first go to his trusted friends, asking for their counsel, not simply their agreement. First he went to Pitt.

Pitt wanted Wilberforce as a political ally, especially with his recently improving reputation. So he asked Wilberforce to stay in politics. But the advice of one person, even a significant person, wasn't enough to convince Wilberforce. Wrestling with his conscience, he sought out John Newton, the author of the hymn "Amazing Grace." Surely he would understand his desire to pursue the ministry. Instead, Newton counseled him as Pitt had, encouraging him to use his political know-how to champion good causes.

No one knows just how much Wilberforce struggled to open his life to the commentary and counsel of others. But it could not have been easy. How do we know? How many people have you approached with the desires of your heart, asking them to provide counsel on whether those desires make sense or not? How many people have asked you to comment on their life purpose or destiny lately? Further, how many folks do you know who have gone as far as Wilberforce, following the advice of others even while disagreeing with it? We all know the line from *For Whom the Bell Tolls*, "No man is an island." But so many of us function as if we were islands, only occasionally allowing others to explore the resources we possess.

Strangely enough, our distaste for vulnerability may strike us deepest after a profound experience on the first rung. Once we have come to the point of trusting God with our destiny, we may jump to conclusions about our life's calling, choosing to do things inconsistent with our capacities or character. There are many who would encourage us to leave our careers and enter into more "spiritual" causes, but this may be just the opposite of God's intent.

"It's amazing how few people know what they are good at," Peter Drucker told Harriet Rubin of *Inc.* magazine. "What comes easy one tends to disparage. If it comes easy, value it. One thinks that what comes hard is more valuable because you have to work at it."[1] Sometimes the only way we can see our talents objectively is through the eyes of others.

Conquering the Fears Within

Choosing vulnerability is tough work. We may not like what people say. We may disagree. Or, for some, the crisis may come when others agree with us—recognizing our true talents and character.

Bill once mentored a man who faced this crisis. Austin excelled in sports throughout his college years. Bill would work out with him from time to time, struggling to keep up and breathing heavily. Austin also excelled academically, which led to his having some great career options.

After launching into his career, Austin climbed through the ranks rather quickly. But when the chief executive invited him to join the top brass, Austin turned him down, causing confusion among his peers and superiors, who had watched his rapid climb to the top with awe. Then he decided to leave the company altogether, even though those closest to him believed he was perfectly matched for such a career.

When Bill quizzed him about this, Austin brushed it aside, at least for awhile. Later Austin confided that his choice frustrated and confused him. "How could I have given up such an opportunity?"

The more they talked, over time, it became clear that Austin didn't feel "worthy" of being among the top brass or in any leadership position. As they talked about his life, they began to notice a pattern. The closer Austin grew to positions of authority and influence, the more nervous and fearful he became. Bill asked him if he thought he could handle the positions he had turned down. He responded yes without any doubts. But Austin was afraid of the recognition and honor, choosing each time to "humbly" decline.

Caught in a false view of humility that was rooted deep in his personal belief system and upbringing, Austin made choices contrary to his abilities and potential and then lived with the pain of his lost opportunities. Although he looked fearless to others on the outside, Austin struggled with deep fears on the inside.

If only Austin had been able to talk through his fears *before the opportunities were lost,* maybe he could have made the right decisions! So you see how vulnerability not only develops character but also produces much better choices on the capacity ladder.

Starbucks CEO Howard Schultz recognized the need for vulnerability when he offered this advice:

> Once you've figured out what you want to do, find someone who has done it before. . . . If they share your values and aspirations, and if they freely share their counsel, they can help you through rough patches and celebrate your victories as their own. That's the kind of mentor I never had as a kid or as a young adult. If one doesn't find you, beat the bushes till you find one who will take you on. And with the right mentor, don't be afraid to expose your vulnerabilities. Admit you don't know what you don't know. When you acknowledge your weaknesses and ask for advice, you'll be surprised how much others help.[2]

Standing on Authentic Humility

Whether we agree or disagree with others' advice, choosing to step up to vulnerability cannot happen without one foot firmly planted on the rung beneath. We must trust God and find others who can be trusted implicitly before we can take such a bold step. Hard as it may seem, taking such a step brings us closer to our destiny. But it cannot be a once-and-done or casual practice.

For instance, Wilberforce chose vulnerability over and over again. After a time of doubt and reflection, he did decide to stay in politics. But then he came under others' influence again, asking friends to help him choose which issues to focus on. Slavery rose as the top issue. Soon thereafter, he decided to recruit others near his hometown of Clapham, gathering regularly with the goal of mutual vulnerability and support. His vulnerability wasn't a passing fad. It became a pattern of his life as he consistently opened his heart to the influence of others. As a result of coming under the influence of others, Wilberforce is remembered as the great reformer whose work led to the abolition of slavery in the British Empire.

Beyond Transparency

Vulnerability does not mean transparency. Transparency is simply disclosing yourself to others at times and in ways that you choose. Although transparency is a good start, in vulnerability you deliberately place yourself under others' influence, submitting yourself to others' strengths. You give others the right to know the pain of your weaknesses and to care for you. You choose to let others know you, to have access to your life, to teach you, and to influence you.

In part, this true vulnerability is what the Bible means when it speaks of submission. *Submission* is a love word, not a control word. Submission means letting someone love you, teach you, or influence you. In fact, the degree to which we submit to others is the degree to which we will experience their love, regardless of how much love they have for us. Submission goes hand in hand with vulnerability.

Many leaders disclose multiple areas of difficulty in their lives (such as problems with impatience, anger, and the like) only when they can maintain control of how they do so or provided they don't have to let others have access to those areas. Indeed, the more eloquent a leader, the more skillfully he or she may be selectively transparent—a clever means of remaining isolated. However, when people allow others to care for their needs—when they submit to others' love—they discover that vulnerability both expresses and sustains integrity.

When Bruce was in his late twenties, an esteemed board of a growing organization invited him to join their team. However, five friends objected and blocked that appointment. As members of the organization, they did not trust his leadership to the point of letting Bruce become a director. This rejection became one of life's most painful circumstances as Bruce thought, "My friends have turned on me." Yet the event became his "turning point" lesson in vulnerability. He chose to go to each of these friends and hear their counsel on what they perceived to be his weaknesses, even though he knew this action would not reverse the hurtful decision. Why did Bruce choose vulnerability?

Defining Integrity

Let's look at the progression. Vulnerability causes people to know your life is open to them. You are teachable. You will allow the cracks in your life to be not only seen but also filled as you receive their influence. This process expresses your integrity to others, and it helps sustain your integrity.

Notice that vulnerability triggers two relational effects. First, people gain access to your life as you submit to their influence. Second, you are given access to their lives as they trust you and see that your life is open to them. What do we call this kind of relationship? *Authenticity*. The kind you can sink your teeth into.

We trust people with authentic integrity. Unlike "silent alarm," "resident alien," "civil war," and "open secret," authentic integrity is not an oxymoron. Some people see integrity as that somewhat annoying aspect of their character that stands in the way of their getting what they might otherwise want. It keeps the married from wandering after other attractive mates. It keeps people from cheating on their taxes. It keeps the cupcakes on the cooling rack and out of our grumbling stomachs before supper. But integrity is much more than this.

In one sense, integrity is an uncompromising adherence to truth. The Hebrew concept of integrity includes straightness, as opposed to crookedness. This meaning has carried forward to our day. Crooked people lack integrity. Stealing from an employer makes you a crook.

Many pursue an uncompromising adherence to truth for its own sake, however, as if this brand of integrity could differentiate them from the common person. We've all met people like this. Integrity is seen by such folk as a badge to be worn. But pursuing integrity solely as a virtue is futile, even destructive to authentic integrity, especially when such people try to shine their integrity badge on the tattered garments of others' character flaws.

The trust others have in us depends on our level of integrity. Integrity is essential to trust. It elicits trust. Pursuing integrity is not just for our benefit. It doesn't earn us any extra credit. Instead, integrity must be pursued as a heart quality that enables us to be love givers and truth tellers among those we influence. Our integrity is always for the benefit of those we influence. And vulnerability expresses and sustains such integrity.

Expanding Influence and Productivity

So as we take this second step up the character ladder we must remember, first, that vulnerability means coming under another's influence, submitting to the love they offer; and second, that vulnerability both expresses and sustains integrity, which earns the trust others need in order to submit to our care. Earning the trust of others leads to a natural third result: vulnerability expands influence and productivity. How does that happen?

Consider how the potential mentor, to whom we alluded earlier in this chapter, lost the substantial influence he could have had with Bruce. Because of this person's isolation, Bruce simply could not trust him, and his influence declined.

Consider also an educated and eloquent Alexandrian debater, who thoroughly knew the Scriptures yet nevertheless submitted to correction in these very areas from a Jewish businessman and a businesswoman from Italy. The man, Apollos, sensed his weakness. More than that, he became vulnerable to the couple, Priscilla and Aquila. His vulnerability caused them to trust him with teaching and with people, and they encouraged others to welcome his teaching and influence.[3] Vulnerability does indeed lead to expanded influence and productivity.

Think about Bruce's five friends again, the ones who rejected his board nomination. Consider the amount of productive work that can be accomplished by them and Bruce in authentic relationships, compared to the fragmented relationships to which isolation would have led. Now multiply that work by thousands of organizations and key leadership relationships that have been forfeited, and you have some idea of the importance of vulnerability in reaching our destiny.

Running from Life on the Run

Vulnerability leads us into seemingly dangerous places. Vulnerability means things like *unguarded, unsafe, defenseless, naked,* and *susceptible*. Little wonder so many leaders skip vulnerability! Why should we open ourselves to the possibility of more pain? Because God accomplishes awesome work in those dangerous places, including deepening the leader's integrity, enlarging the leader's influence, and proving God's ultimate protection of the leader—protection that can make vulnerability safe. And this vulnerability is key to the understanding and release of our strengths for the benefit of others—to knowing who we really are and being truly known by others.

When people exhibit proficiency in leadership, others begin to "look up" to them. Unfortunately, the more others look up to these leaders, the greater the potential for the leaders to end up isolated. Why?

The greater the degree of influence, the greater the potential for a leader to lead a lonely and hidden existence, where people only see what the leader wants them to see. As leaders increase in stature, a significant temptation draws them like a magnet. They are seduced into hiding the truth about themselves in order to create or maintain an image that they believe will maintain their influence. To maintain their position of leadership, people at the top may live lives of pretense and disguise, especially when faced with potential failure, which must be covered up at all costs in order to protect their authority and power. But it doesn't have to be this way.

People need models to follow. But sometimes the pedestals on which people place leaders get dangerously high and fragile. Such pedestals are created when followers place false expectations on a leader, or when leaders place false expectations on themselves. Both contribute to an environment that encourages a lack of vulnerability in leaders. What we really need are models of environments where vulnerability can flourish.

Finding Shelter

Many environments discourage vulnerability. Modern leadership models have failed—big time—in this area. Issues like trust, vulnerability, and integrity often rise to the surface in the debate over new leadership strategies, but debates rarely change relational practices. Out of fear of abuse, control, or manipulation, people are seldom honored for their vulnerability, even in religious circles.

A classic example of resistance to vulnerability occurred between two people, Harry and Katie, good friends who entered into a business venture together. During the startup period, Harry fell ill with a debilitating disease that left him bedridden for weeks at a time. So Katie picked up the slack, making important decisions that couldn't wait and pushing forward as she thought best.

Many months after the startup, Harry's business manager was able to arrange a meeting to discuss the venture. Harry came to the table with a list of issues he felt Katie had overlooked or mishandled during his illness. Katie came to the table with a list of issues Harry knew nothing about, because of her one-sided management of the venture.

Within minutes the air became charged with accusations and anger. Harry began charging Katie with making dishonest and faulty decisions, questioning her motives and integrity. Katie responded by blaming Harry for not being available when she called, questioning *his* motives and integrity. The meeting degenerated into discussions about splitting the partnership until Katie finally blew up and stormed out of the room, vowing that Harry would be hearing from her lawyers.

The business manager took a deep breath and thought, *What just happened?*

A few days later, the business manager met with Katie and challenged her. "Katie, I don't know whose perception of the deal is right or wrong, and frankly, I'm not sure it matters. What matters the most is that I'm hearing that each of you has a great deal of respect and admiration for the other. Yet something is standing between you. Can you think about that and then get back to me before calling your lawyers?"

"Sure," Katie said, "but I don't see how that will help."

The wise business manager scheduled another meeting between Harry and Katie a week later. When Katie walked into the room, she looked directly at Harry and said: "I have a confession to make. Harry, I've got a real problem with anger. I've had the problem all my life and now it's interfering with our friendship and this venture. I can't keep letting my anger rule my life. I'm sorry about how I handled the last meeting."

If that wasn't surprising enough, Harry's response took Katie and the business manager by surprise. "Well, I have a confession to make too. I have this problem with expecting too much from people, and I guess I'm as much to blame for that last meeting as you."

They both realized that not only was their friendship salvageable, but so was the joint venture—at least for the time being. Because both were willing to open their lives up to each other, they could move forward with renewed energy and commitment, without the encumbrance of letting their pride and weaknesses rule the day. They discovered the shelter of each other by choosing vulnerability. (Unfortunately, it didn't last. Within weeks, Katie's anger flared again, but this time she would not relent. The venture and their relationship fell apart.)

Penetrating Invulnerable Leadership Models

The top-down, pyramid-shaped, power-based leadership model can crush vulnerability. It can subtly or overtly impose an isolated existence on people at the top, separating them from those closest to them and alienating them from those who would have the greatest potential to speak into their lives.

Such invulnerable leadership models, along with the unhealthy isolation engendered by their lack of trust, always creates an environment in which character development is at risk. In any culture where people lead at the cost of character, their failure, and the effect of their failure on those they influence, will always be profound. Sometimes the negative impact persists for years, either directly or indirectly. Penetrating such models with grace always starts small. It starts with the choices we make every day.

Ken remembers going to a staff meeting after a conference a while back. As in most companies, at staff meetings people typically ask each other the innocuous question, "How are you?" Except this time, Ken's teammates prodded for a truthful response rather than the typical small-talk answer. But Ken balked. He didn't want them to know how tired and weak and weary he was, although all this showed clearly in his work, attitude, and physical demeanor. Ken still wanted to appear strong. But they asked again, "How are you really?"

He hesitated, not sure what they would say if he admitted his weakness. But because he trusted them, he figured, *What have I got to lose?* So Ken told them how deeply tired he was, so tired he couldn't think straight. He tried to explain how he felt without being embarrassed, but he couldn't. Being vulnerable was so unfamiliar to him in a "corporate" setting.

This is how his team responded. One staff member said, "We believe you. How can we help?"

Another said, "I know how we can help. You need to take some time off. When's the last time you and your wife just took off alone together?"

Still another offered, "Will you let me plan the trip for you?"

They identified Ken's need to be believed. They identified his need for rest. They identified his need to have the details taken care of. (Ken is lousy at planning time off.) They responded with acceptance, affirmation, and with tangible offers of assistance.

In such an environment, with such relationships, you would think that allowing oneself to be vulnerable would be easy, but we assure you it is not. Doing so is always a choice. And sometimes the advice and counsel and observations of others can be hard to hear. But the payback is huge, especially when we follow our vulnerability with the next step, described in the following chapter.

Moving Up

The first rung is *trust God and others with me*. The second is *choose vulnerability*. The second depends on the first. And the third depends on the second. We must pursue intentional vulnerability, both individually and corporately, to go above and beyond our personal best. The world needs vulnerable leaders—people willing to take the risk of opening their lives to the influence of others. And to find or develop this kind of leader we need to seek out and create environments that encourage such vulnerability. Environments where people know their hearts will not be sacrificed for an agenda—inappropriately called success. Are you ready to live in such an environment? Are you ready to begin building one?

Are you tired of living in the "dark wood," feeling isolated and lost though surrounded by others? Do you know two or more people whom you trust implicitly? Are you willing to come under their influence in a much deeper way than you ever thought possible? Are you ready to be vulnerable enough to earn their trust? Becoming vulnerable will both enhance your integrity and express it to others. Does this appeal to you? If so, call those people. Write them. Schedule a time to get together and tell them what's in your heart. Choose vulnerability and then get ready for the next rung.

Grabbing Hold

- What causes you to fear vulnerability?
- Are you willing to trust others with your vulnerability to avoid isolation?
- How do you protect and care for those who have been vulnerable with you?

Chapter Seven

The Third Rung

Aligning with Truth

Whenever two people meet there are really six
people present. There is each man as he sees
himself, each as the other person sees him, and
each man as he really is.

—*William James*

At the early age of twenty-four, a floundering Vincent van Gogh received a letter from his elder brother Theo, strongly encouraging him to become an artist. Although others had already begun to treat Vincent's passionate leanings with skepticism, Theo understood him best and remained his closest confidant and ally. Still, Vincent refused his brother's advice. Instead, he left a promising career as an art dealer and began studying to become a teacher. A harmful pattern had begun.

Within the year, it became apparent to all that Vincent would not make it through the rigorous training required of teachers. He had neither the temperament nor the talent for it. Again he asked Theo for advice. But against the urgings of Theo, his parents, and other near relatives, Vincent decided to become an evangelist. The harmful pattern continued.

What pattern? If his sister-in-law's analysis is true—and from Vincent's own letters it appears to be—van Gogh had a difficult time receiving the counsel and concern of others. It seems Vincent had a warped view of humility. It sounds harsh to say it, but as religious as he was, instead of trusting God and others with himself, he trusted only himself with himself. How do we know this? Because he refused others' counsel, particularly the counsel of those who loved him and cared about him. No matter what a person's chosen vocation, this behavior is a sign not of spiritual maturity but of well-masked pride and arrogance.

Some, like Vincent, believe they can simply maintain a vertical relationship with God while avoiding the horizontal relationships of everyday human interaction. They believe they can experience all that God has for them without receiving the love of others. They may even call this superior spirituality. But though certain religious sects may support isolationist spirituality by tradition, there is little in the Bible to support this. In fact, we would do well to examine the life of Jesus. By his example, he soundly repudiates such a lifestyle. He chose intentionally to live and work with twelve fallible and very ordinary men. He allowed several women, such as Mary and Martha of Bethany, and even a prostitute, Mary Magdalene, to minister to his needs. Jesus himself chose being vulnerable over a lifestyle of isolation. But van Gogh recoiled from such vulnerability.

As his romantic ideals of personal isolation and rugged individualism held sway, Vincent chose to abandon virtually all his relationships, save the one with Theo (by a fragile thread), almost starving himself to death in the impoverished coal town of the Borinage. Refusing to heed Theo's ongoing insights into his artistic gift and rejecting the counsel of the church leaders about his service, van Gogh wallowed in self-pity about his failures. His remorse brought him to the point of abandoning his faith, thoroughly disappointed in the God who had not rewarded his self-denial and seemingly pure aspirations to love his fellow humans. Oddly enough, he never considered that God, rather than abandoning him, had perhaps been speaking to him all along through those who loved him.

The Lost Art of Listening

Seeking the counsel of those who know and love us is a good practice on both ladders. On the capacity ladder, when we reach the point at which we become aware of our talents, it is a good thing to ask questions: Do I show promise as an artist? Can I do the math it takes to be an engineer? When we refuse such vulnerability, we can miss our calling altogether, unless we stumble upon it much later in life, as Vincent did.

In a particularly dark moment, he wrote to Theo, "I said to myself, I'll take up my pencil again, I will take up drawing, and from that moment everything has changed for me."

He had finally found his calling. But in doing so, he abandoned the relationships he longed for and needed to climb the character ladder, including his relationship with the Caller. As a result, his capacities for creating art became a curse to him instead of a blessing. Throughout his artistic career, Vincent persisted in ignoring the advice of those who cared deeply for him, leaving a trail of broken, reckless relationships in his wake. He pursued his painting with a commitment bordering on madness. Obsessed with his ideas, he demanded that people accept his terms for living and loving. His lonely life became representative of the romantic notion of the "starving artist"—a person misunderstood and unloved by an antagonistic culture.

One tragedy of van Gogh's career was his refusal to accept the guidance of others in his capacities, in particular the guidance of those who *did* understand and encourage him in his art. Had he listened to those whom he could trust, like Theo, he would have begun painting much earlier in life, avoiding the frustrations and pain of choosing unwisely. But this wasn't the greatest tragedy.

Starving for Love

Van Gogh certainly made his mark on the world of art, but he never reached his goal of living selflessly for others. According to Vincent's sister-in-law, "It was his aim to humble himself, to forget himself, to sacrifice every personal desire—that was the ideal he tried to reach as long as he sought his refuge in religion, and he never did a thing by halves. But to follow the paths trodden by others, to submit to the will of other people, that was not in his character, he wanted to work out his own salvation."[1]

Vincent, a bitter and lonely person, ended his own life with a bullet. He could not work out his own salvation. He could not love others because he was not fulfilled himself. He would not allow God or others to meet his deepest needs. This was the greatest tragedy.

Imagine what van Gogh could have produced had he found his ideal of a "plein air" community of artists pursuing art for the common man. Unfortunately, his attempts stumbled over his desire to control and manipulate the lives of others. He drove people away from him, Paul Gauguin being the most memorable example. He would not allow them to address his personality flaws, weaknesses, or poor habits. His art didn't bring him down. His heart did.

Aligning with Truth

The character ladder is not as concerned with what we do as it is with who we are. Its emphasis is on human "being" more than human "doing." Instead of the What questions, it asks the Why questions. Why do I want this job? Why do I want to do this thing? Why do I think my life would be better if only . . . ? Chances are, if van Gogh had allowed himself to address the Why questions, his story could have ended much differently. He could have gone above and beyond his individual best and reached God's best for his life, actually leaving the legacy of love, humility, and selfless service he earnestly desired in his younger years.

When we ascend the first and second rungs of the character ladder, entrusting our needs to God and others and choosing to open our lives for their review, we soon face the next step—the third rung on the character ladder: *align with truth*. On this rung we must ask more soul-searching questions. Will I listen to what they say? Do I believe it is true? Will I follow their advice? (See Figure 7.1.)

This is the true test of character: not just coming under others' influence but acting on the wisdom and truth of their counsel. Aligning with truth distinguishes between those who use transparency to manipulate and those who submit in vulnerability to live lives of integrity.

Figure 7.1. The Third Rung of the Character Ladder

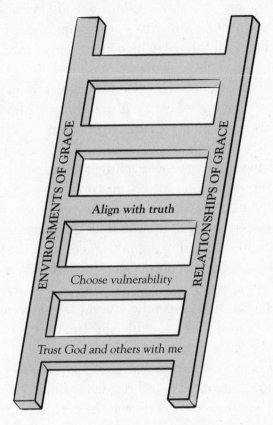

Thinking back to the last chapter, when Bruce's friends rejected his board nomination, what would have happened if after going to them in vulnerability and listening to their counsel, he had then pushed ahead trying to get around their objections? What would have happened if Bruce had simply ignored them, claiming a better knowledge of his abilities and character than they had observed?

But he didn't. He listened intently and looked for the wisdom in their words. Although their critique hurt awhile, his decision to yield to their counsel had far-reaching results. Those five friends now receive Bruce's advice and counsel to their deepest struggles.

Why? Because vulnerability exposes the motive of our heart—to live lives of integrity. And the resulting realignment of our lives convinces others of our integrity—our commitment to adhere to the truth. People will trust us to influence them in ways they never could have if we had chosen differently.

The climb up the character ladder is a climb toward interdependence. With each rung, we escape further from the hungry jaws of an isolated existence and move closer to our destiny. No matter how much people try to romanticize, idolize, or imitate self-protective isolation and angst, leaders, lovers, entrepreneurs, and artists would be far better served by choosing community.

Tim Timmerman also sketched out a plan to live as a fine artist. After his first degree, he put himself through graduate school and began painting and sculpting assemblages of found objects. Tim's unorthodox art touches people deeply. His works have a cathartic, healing quality about them. Often, viewers will be startled as the images and objects stir their psyche, causing forgotten memories to surface—some joyful, some tearful. But Tim's own internal pain could not be cured by his art.

"I kept looking for answers because I knew there had to be something more," he explains. "I needed intimacy, honesty, and healing. I just wanted to be cared for at the core of who I was. Yet I was terrified at the same time. I wanted people to know me, but I didn't like me. In fact, I hated me. So I figured others would too. I thought that if I was vulnerable, I would be killed, because I'd have to throw my safety mechanisms to the wind."

Some friends urged Tim to take a risk and let a group of men inside his life. They came from a variety of backgrounds, faiths, vocations, and age groups, but they shared commitment to honesty, acceptance, vulnerability, and safety. "They gave me an environment where I could be totally naked emotionally," explains Tim. "Before, I wouldn't let people in. I wouldn't believe anybody. But I discovered a principle. It's staying hidden that kills you. To the level I am vulnerable with those guys, they will come back to me with twice as much care and sensitivity. Instead of killing me when I tell them what I really think and feel, they love me all the more."

But meeting with this group of men was not as easy or soft as it may appear. Tim says he knew that each week those men would ask him tough questions. As Tim shared his struggles, they would ply him with questions until his beliefs and defenses were revealed for what they were: truth or lie. They refused to let Tim hide behind lame excuses for running away. The group helped (and still helps) Tim remain vulnerable, and it helps him take the next step by encouraging him to align with truth.

For instance, one day Tim's boss asked him to make some significant changes in the art department that Tim heads. At first, Tim followed his old pattern of self-pity and compliance with his boss's wishes, assuming he could not change the circumstances. But then Tim thought of what he had learned about himself in his men's group, and what he'd say to those men next week after complaining about the actions of his boss. Tim asked himself, "If I have to be dishonest about what I think and feel in order to stay at this school, then what kind of life do I have?" He concluded, "Either I tell my boss what I think, or I have nothing to offer anyway." So Tim walked into his boss's office and objected to the proposed changes, explaining what would happen if he was forced to comply. Tim's curriculum and department remained intact, much to the benefit of his students, the school, and his boss.

The effects of the men's group on Tim's life cannot be overvalued. He found strength he never knew he had. He found it in a community of grace, made up of a diverse group of ordinary people, some with even more hang-ups and pains than he had. Tim says, "I'm not afraid anymore. I sense amazing freedom. The group has moved me to a place where I can love myself, based on the value God placed in me." The strangest thing, according to Tim, is that many of the men in the group don't believe as Tim does, yet they have been instrumental in affirming and strengthening Tim's faith. "They told me, 'You're you for a reason. Stop trying to change you.'" They challenged Tim's acceptance of grace and challenged him on what he said he believed. Through those ordinary men, Tim has learned to take better care of himself and live with greater integrity and freedom.

To align ourselves with truth is a personal decision that is best made in a community of people who care for us. The truth about who we are cannot be wholly known without interaction with others. We all have blind spots that only others can see.

The Johari window, developed by Joe Luft and Harry Ingham, illustrates this point. Each of us has parts of our lives that are known to others and other parts that remain unknown to others. Our lives also have parts that are known to us and other parts that are unknown to us. Others' perceptions can be particularly helpful to us in the areas where we are blind—where others perceive things in us that we cannot perceive in ourselves. Many of their perceptions in this area have to do with our character. Figure 7.2 illustrates how our becoming vulnerable affects the Johari window.

Although many capacities can be developed outside of intimate, authentic relationships, character cannot. We need community, a concept that Westerners may overlook in their preoccupation with the individual.

Yardsticks

To align with truth requires a standard of measure. We have become a culture possessed by the authority of tests. Our current educational system seems to rest on the assumption that life change can occur through learning without practical application in the context of community. Our society measures success by test scores and evaluations rather than by people's ability to apply what they know in the context of relationship.

We have developed IQ tests to measure intelligence, and personality tests to determine leadership style. Recently, we have developed EQ tests to measure our emotional competence. Each time we take a test, we trust the "experts" to analyze us. Our personal growth then becomes a matter of determining our score and appraising ourselves according to statistical means and averages. Typically, an individual collects the data, then stands as judge, jury, defendant, and counsel in her own evaluation. Meant as tools for

Figure 7.2. The Effect of Vulnerability
on the Johari Window

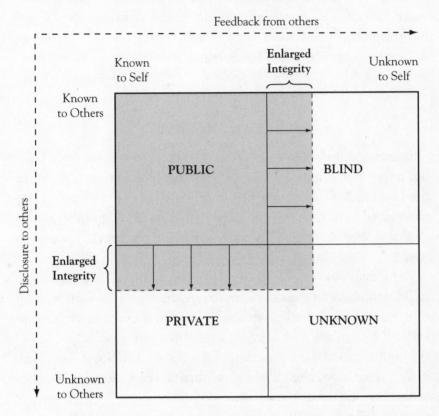

Source: Adapted from Hersey and Blanchard, 1993, p. 299.

personal evaluation in the comfort of our own home or office, such tests can be valuable, but probably much less so than we realize.

The real tests of character have existed since people first walked the earth: Will we trust others? Will we be vulnerable with them? Will we follow their counsel in regard to our character? These things cannot be measured or developed in isolation. They can only be measured and developed in relationship with others. What we discover about ourselves increases in value when we share the results with trusted friends and they agree with our discoveries. But we will learn even more about ourselves if those friends disagree. We will also make valuable discoveries about our friends in the process of working through our disagreements. In other words, if we believe we have mature character but haven't asked a friend about it, we probably don't.

Ultimate Standards

Ultimately, our standards for character should not come from tests, but rather from God. We can think of the Ten Commandments or the Golden Rule as representing standards of truth. A man once confronted Jesus with the question, "What must I do to inherit eternal life?" Jesus answered, "What is written in the Law? How do you read it?"

The man answered correctly with the traditional Shema recited by Jews throughout the centuries: "Love the Lord your God with all your heart and with all your soul and with all your strength and with all your mind, and, love your neighbor as yourself."[2]

Jesus affirmed the man's correct answer as the ultimate standard. In fact, Jesus had recited the Shema himself when asked by a teacher of the law, "What is the greatest commandment?" When we ask what truth we must align with, we must remember that "all the Law and the Prophets hang on these two commandments" to love God and love others.[3] We must also remember the conversation that followed between the young man and Jesus.

Jesus exhorted, "Do this and you will live." But the man wasn't interested in acting on the truth he knew; instead, he tried to avoid alignment by asking, "And who is my neighbor?" Jesus then told the parable of the Good Samaritan, in which a man from a despised race demonstrated love far better than the religious leaders who claimed to live by the truth.

The young man, like most of us, understood the truth intellectually but wanted to define his own terms for the expression of love. We do the same when we wonder, You don't mean I have to accept *that* person, do you? You don't mean I should help her out instead of just firing her? or, You don't mean I should stick it out after what he did to me?

The Bible just doesn't offer explicit answers to the barrage of "gray" decisions we face each day. We want to love. We want to be loved. Still, like van Gogh, most of us don't know how to gauge how well we're doing, and when faced with God's standard, we tend to lower it to one that is easier to execute.

One thing is for sure: when we are left to our own judgment of ourselves, it becomes pretty easy to overlook or excuse misalignments for the sake of what the capacity ladder seems to offer. We may hide behind our own versions of "Who is my neighbor?" in an attempt to avoid friction that could cause positive adjustments in our own lives. We may just keep adopting a lower standard for our relationships while giving assent to a higher standard in our minds.

Upper and Lower Stories

In Hebrew philosophy, a belief was not a belief until it was acted on. And all beliefs affected community, because the actions they spawned affected every area of life. In Greek philosophy, belief could be separated from action. Thought and action suffered a painful divorce into upper and lower stories of existence.

Greek thinking led to dualism, a separation between the material and spiritual aspects of life. The material world—the realm of the senses and action—declined in value. The spiritual world—the realm of the mind and emotions—represented a higher plane of existence. The work of earning daily bread played second fiddle to the pursuit of philosophy. Greek thought infiltrated the early church and gave birth to a separate class of priests, clerics, and a host of monastic orders. This thinking still pervades modern society and the church in a variety of ways.

The Hebrew philosophy seems comparatively simple. No dualism. No separation. If you love someone, you will meet her need. If you meet someone's need, you love her. Hebrews did not separate the heart from the mind, or belief from action. They were one and the same. What you believed affected all you did, from cooking a meal to building a city. What you did reflected what you believed. Therefore, work became an act of worship, and no vocation was viewed as more sacred or higher than another.

How does all this relate to the character ladder? First, when we adopt the Hebrew viewpoint, we recognize just how integrated each step of the ladder is. There can be no true humility—trusting God with me—without an act of vulnerability. There can be no vulnerability without a corresponding alignment with truth.

Second, the Hebrew philosophy leaves no room for an isolated existence. Each step of the ladder requires application in the context of relationship. We cannot trust God or others, choose vulnerability, or align with truth without relationships, because without community, these become sterile principles or intellectual exercises providing no real benefit to anyone.

To say we have chosen to align our lives with truth while remaining isolated from others and invulnerable to their guidance and love is a sure sign that our destiny is in jeopardy. To enter into relationships of trust, come under the influence of those people, and then follow through on what they say is a sure sign that we are heading for something better.

Obedience Versus Compliance

In addition to dualistic thinking, there is another hazard we face on the third rung, stemming from a subtle misunderstanding of alignment. Max De Pree, former chairman and CEO of Herman-Miller, wrote, "Each of us, no matter what our rank in the hierarchy may be, has the same rights: to be needed, to be involved, to have a covenantal relationship, to understand the corporation, to affect our destiny, to be accountable, to appeal, to make a commitment."[4] Each of these rights comes with implied responsibilities. To protect these rights, someone must determine how they will be expressed and upheld within a community or corporation.

A well-functioning group will establish rules of cooperation—rules to guide people and coordinate their activities in ways that protect individual and corporate rights. Therefore, to be a responsible citizen of a particular group, one must obey the rules of the group. Disobedience implies that one either does not care to protect someone else's rights, or that one thinks the rules are unjust. When the rules of cooperation serve to perpetuate the violation of someone's rights—to be needed, involved, educated, able to appeal, accountable, or committed—the rules are unjust, because they violate the deeper rule to love God and to love others.

To be sure, alignment implies cooperation. To align means to bring into agreement or accord. In the case of the character ladder, alignment implies a certain harmony with others. Like a group of musicians, community requires give-and-take among a variety of relational roles: peer to peer, leader to follower, and follower to leader. Communities with no rules of cooperation turn into a harsh cacophony of competing sounds. Communities with too many rules of cooperation, or unjust ones, may make music—but mostly boring, unimaginative funeral dirges. Just as any musical group must obey certain rules of cooperation, so any community or corporation must create and follow guidelines to enable each person to express his or her uniqueness amid diversity.

In some roles, responsible group members must obey the leader's direction. In other roles, we should expect others to obey our lead. Sometimes the authority structure needed to define and uphold the rules of cooperation can seem to infringe on our personal rights. In this case, it becomes the leader's responsibility to pay attention and respond appropriately to those who feel the injustice. Leaders must never assume that one's compliance with the rules means one fully agrees or wishes to cooperate with the rules. On the character ladder, we must never mistake "alignment to please" with "alignment with truth," either in our own responses to authority figures or in other's responses to our authority. To create fair and gracious rules of cooperation—the kind that facilitate environments and relationships of grace—we must avoid mistaking compliance for obedience.

Bruce once had an able administrative assistant who served his company well for several years. It rarely occurred to Bruce to solicit her counsel on organizational and relational decisions, even though he routinely asked the advice of executives, some of whom had less awareness of organizational history, relationships, and potential.

As Bruce learned later, for years this person had dutifully implemented plans that conflicted with her better judgment and intuition. Only when she left the company for another did Bruce learn she had been executing his plans with increasing indifference. She told Bruce that it was not his selection of plans contrary to her opinion that disheartened her. Rather, she grew increasingly passive as Bruce failed to honor her insight and substantial perspective. He had nurtured compliance in this valuable partner.

Because of rights abuses, obedience has a bad reputation in many circles. But the kind of obedience needed to align with truth is an obedience that comes from the heart. Obedience from the heart does not mean setting aside our God-given right to question or appeal. It does not mean giving up our right to affect our own destiny. And it certainly was never intended to strip us of our sense of ownership in the work of our hands. Obedience from the heart does not mean a loss of self. Obedience from the heart does not mean compliance.

Compliance sounds like, "OK, OK. I'll do it. But it won't be pretty." Obedience from the heart says, "I'll do this because I trust you and believe it is for our best." Aligning with truth flows from a heart that obeys in trust. Compliance simply concedes to oppression. Compliance, even when it takes the form of serving others, typically turns into some form of rebellion or resentment. Obedience from the heart develops trust and acceptance. When faced with failure, compliant people blame others, particularly their leaders. When faced with negative consequences, obedient people—those who align with truth with all their hearts—own the consequences with those who have influenced them, most often their leaders.

It may sound to some people as though the obedience implied in alignment with truth excuses them from personal responsibility, because they are simply doing what others ask or tell them to. Compliant people tend to hide behind the choices others make for their lives. Alignment with truth means nothing of the sort.

The obedience inherent in alignment with truth presupposes that we will exercise our God-given rights, some of which De Pree mentions. We will question when we do not understand, and we will give others the chance to question. We will make personal commitments to others' plans, and we will allow others to express the degree of their commitment to our plans. Alignment requires mutual, supportive, accountable relationships in an environment where such values can be honored.

Bill Pollard once confronted this problem early in his career at ServiceMaster. While preparing the books for year-end closing, the outside auditors discovered that a small kickback had been paid in an overseas unit reporting directly to Pollard. Digging into the circumstances, he found an intentional cover-up whereby employees had been fired or shut down through fear and intimidation tactics.

Pollard says he learned a powerful lesson: "I had failed to dip far enough into the organization to sense this problem. In the process of listening to all the good reports, people had not been encouraged or empowered to be open about the wrongs and the mistakes. We had conditioned people to look the other way and not own a result to the extent of being a part of the correction process."[5] Pollard had learned the dangers of allowing an organization to drift into compliance, a situation in which the God-given rights of people are violated and alignment with truth is devalued and thwarted.

Flame of Glory

Another obstacle often causes people to slip from the third rung. We call it the "flame of glory" syndrome. It stems from lack of hope or from fear of being controlled. Some people adopt as their slogan something like a line from an old Neil Young song: "It's better to burn out than to fade away." Convinced that they cannot handle the counsel of others, they cannot obey the rules of cooperation, they cannot change themselves, or they cannot change their environment, they exchange what could have been for what they can experience in the present moment. Some may go wild in their pursuit of pleasure. For most, this obstacle takes on a subtler form. "I just want to be happy," one may say when faced with the hard realities of third-rung difficulties. "Can't I just leave here and start over somewhere else? Maybe a farm in the Midwest with nobody around for miles?" Someone who has found success on the capacity ladder may fall victim to indifference, saying something like, "Who needs character or this relationship stuff? I've got it made on the capacity ladder."

Whether it ends up looking like blatant hedonism, wistful isolationism, or anything in between, the flame-of-glory syndrome stems from the fanciful notion that doing things our way—to bring the greatest pleasure right now, no matter what the consequences—has inherent value. "Follow your heart," some may say, or "If it feels good, do it." Kierkegaard described such people as "aesthetes." M. E. Zimmerman summarizes Kierkegaard's description of people who succumb to flame-of-glory thinking: "Since for him there is no sense that he belongs to past or future, time becomes a series of now-moments which must be filled with pleasurable distractions. Although thus bound to the present, he is not satisfied with what it offers. . . . There is never enough time for anything. He races through life thinking that—as each minute ticks away—he is missing out on gratification. . . . Because he is constantly fleeing from disclosure of his own mortality . . . , [he] elects to remain locked in his own ego."[6]

Those who succumb to flame-of-glory thinking usually end up hurting their communities and themselves. They settle for what they can get on their own, rather than what they can give and receive in community with others.

The flame-of-glory syndrome, at its core, is glorified ego gratification. It may hide under the veneer of pop philosophy or mass marketing, but ultimately this selfish tendency lures us all at some time or another. Some bounce from place to place, looking for the ultimate job, church, or relationship. Others leave behind spouses and children in their pursuit of something they cannot quite define. Our cultural symbolism, as in John Wayne movies for instance, even reinforces such behavior.

Still, at some point, we have each wanted to be our own boss, be somebody else's boss, or perhaps even say what one character says in an Ashleigh Brilliant cartoon: "Use your own judgment, then do as I say," or in another quip of his, "Do your best to satisfy me—that's all I ask of everybody."[7] We struggle with selfishness because we fear what others might say or do to us if we offer them our vulnerability, and we think we could do better on our own. We struggle to hear the truth because we're not so sure listening to the truth will feel good or be much fun. We struggle to obey the truth from the heart because we fear we'll be hurt in the process. It doesn't take much imagination to come up with reasons to jump or slip off the character ladder at this point.

But there are just as many reasons to strengthen your grip and hold on tight. Yet without relationships of acceptance and trust, people lose hope. When people lose hope, they become easy to control. When people are easy to control, others with faulty character have a field day, preying on the hearts of the hopeless through false promises, false doctrine, and false experiences. Although they aim to control their own destiny, such people are more out of control and under the control of others than they realize. They are trapped in unfulfillment in a way that makes them vulnerable to every hollow promise of fulfillment that comes along.

The Path to Fulfillment

Our lives don't have to be this way. We do not have to give up community, our families, and our relationships in order to find fulfillment. People should not be sacrificed on the altar of our capacity-ladder ascent. Our lives can value and honor relationships and still release our potential. Indeed, reaching for destiny in harmony with others will not hinder our potential; rather, it will fulfill it in ways we could never have imagined.

No slippery obstacle—not dualistic thinking, not false assumptions, not compliance, not the flame-of-glory syndrome—as slick as it may seem, can force us off the third rung when we live in trusting, vulnerable communities that radiate the aura of grace.

Do you, like van Gogh, long for such a community? Do you want to know others and be known by them? Do you long to love and be loved as you reach for your dreams? As we've said, climbing the character ladder is not easy. But once you've known the joy of having a small circle of friends share your burden, "easy" becomes less important when compared to experiencing fulfillment. Once you've experienced the wisdom of making a good choice, having far more confidence that it is a right choice, you'll wonder how you got along before. And you'll be ready for the next rung.

Grabbing Hold

- With whom do you intentionally share your needs? Which relationships have helped you mature?

- In what ways have you ignored advice that could have helped you?

- Which heart attitude dominates your choices: obedience from the heart, or compliance?

- Do you encourage obedience or compliance in your leadership?

Chapter Eight

The Fourth Rung

Paying the Price

Courage is not the absence of fear, but rather the
judgment that something else is more important
than fear.

—*Ambrose Redmoon*

At least five companies answered the alarm, and still they couldn't
squelch the flames of the aging hotel. As one firefighter ascended an
extension ladder, he viewed the chaos below. Sirens wailed. Media
hounds pressed closer for better photos. The chief shouted orders
through a megaphone. While water pelted the firefighter, spotlights
focused on his bright yellow slicker, lighting his way through the
smoky blackness of the night sky. He kept climbing closer to the
raging flames, knowing that people's lives depended on his courage.

The firefighter had been trained to keep his cool in such hot situations. But something happened about three-fifths of the way up
that ladder. He froze. He just couldn't make his legs take one more
step. With the chaos below and the impending danger above, something inside him snapped. All the reason and courage he could
muster would not thaw his fear. The paparazzi's cameras also snapped,
recording his anxious and humiliating moment for posterity.

Sometimes the character ladder can cause such moments, particularly on the final rungs. They may be subtler, but the feelings
come very close to those of the firefighter. Fear tugs at the heart,
keeping leaders from continuing their climb, even though many
could benefit from their continuing ascent.

As Bruce Laingren discovered back in 1979–1981, while undergoing the rigors of 444 days as a hostage in Iran, "Human beings are like tea bags. You don't know your own strength until you get into hot water."[1]

Fourth-Rung Fears

On the capacity ladder, our training, experiences, and titles may have catapulted us to the fourth rung. Getting to the fourth rung on the short ladder means we have arrived at the top. In contrast, getting to the fourth rung on the character ladder means we still face some of the toughest challenges. This creates fear and the temptation to escape a gripping tension we experience on this rung.

What is this tension? On the fourth rung of the capacity ladder, we may enjoy certain privileges, power, and authority from our climb, whereas on the fourth rung of the character ladder we come face to face with daily opportunities to set aside those same short-ladder payoffs in order to make profound differences in the lives of others. The tension comes in deciding which to choose, especially when some character-ladder choices require capacity-ladder setbacks. A father may need to cut back on work hours to care for his spouse or family, hurting his chances for a promotion or even jeopardizing his job. A woman who finds that she has chosen the wrong profession for the wrong reasons may find it difficult to sacrifice her current status in order to enter a new phase of personal growth, even if her newfound discovery appears exciting and more aligned with the truth about who she is. This tension creates tremendous pressure to step off the long ladder—to kick back and rest on our laurels awhile. Or, if we attempt the climb, we may freeze from fear as we see what lies ahead.

Those at the top of the capacity ladder face the greatest potential pain or loss in honoring the process of the character ladder. They simply have more to lose than those on the lower capacity rungs.

For instance, if a developing leader confronts a character flaw during her college years, she may experience anxiety when she realizes what it will take to address it. She will have to humbly admit her problem to God and others. She will have to be vulnerable with those she has offended, asking for forgiveness and making amends according to trusted counsel. These are difficult things to do. But just think how fearful she would become trying to deal with her flaw later—after it had continued unchecked for twenty years amid increasing influence and responsibilities!

. It's on the fourth rungs of both ladders that leaders face the greatest challenges from without. Subordinates who covet power or position may use the leaders' weaknesses against them. Competitors wait to pounce on any perceived vulnerability. Critics and detractors abound. It's also on the fourth rungs that leaders face the greatest challenges from *within*. Will I use my power simply to hold on to my position? My privileges? My paycheck? Will I use my authority to hide the truth, to shade the truth, or to redefine the truth about who I am?

Few leaders proactively wrestle with such decisions. Instead, most slowly drift off course. Because of real and supposed threats, they may try to project an image of invulnerability, strength, or rightness to defend themselves. Perhaps they feel they've earned the right to such a defense by power. After all, they worked hard to get where they are. Shouldn't they be able to defend or enjoy what they've earned? Even those who have climbed both ladders, integrating their capacity climb with the character rungs, may get lulled into a stupor once they feel they've reached their capacity goals.

Sieges of the Heart

Ken remembers some verses from a song, "Healing Touch," written by Russ and Tori Taff and James Hollihan, that once helped expose his own stupor:

I stare at the door, trapped in a dream
Held like a captive
By what people see on the outside
They don't really know me[2]

Trapped. Held like a captive. Unknown. You might be surprised by how many people feel the same way, perhaps especially those who have made it to the top of the capacity ladder. But then again, maybe you're not surprised at all. Maybe you have been there or are there now. Many who rise to the fourth rung find themselves in just such a place.

In Ken's case, he had pursued a path toward a goal. The path had run its course. But when he reached the goal, Ken found he had given up too much of what really mattered in order to attain it. He found himself gripped with fear. Again, the song spoke to him:

Shades of the truth locked up in lies
Days run into days
When I open my eyes, see how far it's gone
Where did things go wrong?
Choices were made, dreams were pushed aside
Not so much a conscious thought
But resignation, a siege of the heart
But there's a part that calls to You[3]

Where did things go wrong? What are those things that leaders sometimes resign themselves to—those "sieges of the heart"—that can rob them of their dreams and their destiny? There are many.

We may subtly shift our emphasis from what's best for those under our care to what's best for our ego, elevating the importance of a position above a higher purpose. We may succumb to the myth of arrival, confusing our capacity goals with our ultimate destiny, leading us into arrogance. Or perhaps the worst siege of the heart occurs when we begin to believe we are different, that we cannot be understood by anyone except those in some clique or club, who in fact just affirm our wrong assumptions.

Each of these temptations can keep us frozen on the lower rungs of the character ladder and moving further and further into isolation. Still, as the song lyric says, amid these sieges there is always that "part that calls to You." We still have hope because God's grace can lead us home.

Three Steps Back

You may remember from previous chapters that people trust leaders with integrity. You may also recall that integrity flows from choosing vulnerability and aligning with truth and that both of these stem from leaders' willingness to trust God and others with themselves.

As Figure 8.1 illustrates, these first three rungs of the character ladder—trust God and others with me, choose vulnerability, and align with truth—correspond very closely with three gracious outcomes—humility, submission, and obedience. Relationships and environments of grace call for leaders who possess these three gracious character traits, because relationships and environments of grace require leaders who possess the ability to love. Let us explain.

To experience the benefits of love, people must receive love. For love to be received, the receiver must trust the giver of love. To be trusted, the giver of love must have integrity. To have integrity, the giver of love must submit to others in vulnerability and align with truth in obedience. At the bottom of all this, givers of love must entrust themselves to God in humility.

This long-ladder pattern can be seen quite clearly in the life of Jesus, "who had equal status with God but didn't think so much of himself that he had to cling to the advantages of that status no matter what. Not at all. When the time came, he set aside the privileges of deity and took on the status of a slave, became *human!* Having become human, he stayed human. It was an incredibly humbling process. He didn't claim special privileges. Instead, he lived a selfless, obedient life."[4]

So far, so good. Most of us want to be the kind of leader who will set aside his or her rights for the benefit of others. We want to

Figure 8.1. The Fruit of the First Three Rungs

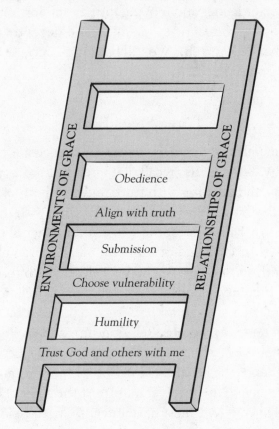

be servant leaders. We may even be encouraged by what followed Jesus' obedience: "God lifted him high and honored him far beyond anyone or anything, ever."[5] Now that's getting to the top!

The Price of Love

Of course, we left out one small but important phrase that came between the "obedience" and the "honor" parts. What did Jesus become obedient to? The part we left out says that he "died a selfless, obedient death—and the worst kind of death at that: a crucifixion."[6] Jesus, the best example of a servant leader, paid a price in order to express God's love to others. On the character ladder, we must also pay a price. What price? Within the boundaries of loving God and loving others, the payment will be different for each of us. God does not have the same plan for everyone. We need only to look to Jesus' leadership to see just how varied the price can be. When a man named Zacchaeus decided to use his great wealth to repay what he had cheated from others, Jesus affirmed him.[7] But Jesus commanded another rich man to sell everything he had and give it to the poor.[8] Jesus asked some people to follow him by leaving their homes and careers behind. Others Jesus told to return to their home towns, despite their pleadings to be allowed to follow him. Some of Jesus' followers lived to a ripe old age. Other disciples died young as martyrs. It would be much easier to count the cost of aligning with truth if we all walked the same path. But we do not.

Some will be asked to devote their lives to the service of others and pay the price of living in obscurity, when a different choice could have brought them fame or fortune. Others will be asked to use their athletic gifts and pay the price of living continuously under the glare of the spotlight. Make no mistake about it, though, there will be a price to pay when we choose to climb the character ladder to the point of aligning with truth. This is why the fourth rung—*pay the price*—can leave us clinging desperately, frozen partway up the longer ladder. "Paying the price" implies something that none of us likes to think about. It implies suffering, much like the smoke and flames faced by the firefighter earlier in the chapter. (See Figure 8.2.)

That firefighter eventually did move from his frightening perch, but only after several of his comrades climbed up to where he was and helped him regain his composure. They reminded him of their assistance in the battle against the flames. They encouraged him by reminding him of the goal of their courage—to save others from death. And they expressed compassion. Each of them knew exactly what he felt at that moment, for they had been there before and had come through it.

We also need friends to support and encourage us, especially on the fourth rung of the character ladder, when we can become anxious

Figure 8.2. The Fourth Rung of the Character Ladder

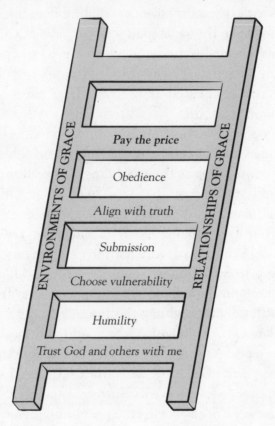

or even immobilized by the price we are asked to pay. Trusted friends who know us and share our values can help us evaluate the costs of our decisions, reminding us of the goal of our climb. Concerned, committed friends who tell us the truth can restore our objectivity—our ability to remain focused on reality. Without objectivity, we may react to a situation based on pain from our past, the crisis of the moment, or fear of the future.

Looking for White

Bill and his wife, Grace, once faced a situation where their need for objectivity became painfully acute. Rain pelted their small plane as gusts of wind tossed them about. Bill and Grace became nervous as their friend Jim, their pilot, asked them to help him "look for white." He explained that a white area in the midst of the ominous black storm surrounding them would lead to the sun. But they couldn't see white anywhere. First Jim tried flying above the storm, but couldn't find a way. Then he tried getting beneath it, but they had to pull up for fear of crashing into the nearby mountain peaks. Bill feared they might not make it.

One of the worst things pilots can do in such a situation is trust their feelings or the view in front of their noses. Those who make such mistakes have found themselves in precarious and even deadly situations. Some pilots have flown upside down without realizing it. Others have misjudged landings by hundreds of feet, ending in disaster. That's why, in the darkest times, Jim turned to his instruments to keep his perspective. Even so, they never did find a way through that storm.

After failing to find a way around or through it, Jim told Bill and Grace he knew where the sun was—behind them. So he turned the plane around and headed back to safety. But without his keeping both objectivity and a close watch on his instrument panel, he could not have kept his cool or even figured out which way was back.

We need to keep our wits about us too, especially amid the storms swirling occasionally around the fourth rung. Those who lose objectivity in the midst of "paying the price" may lose their grip on the character ladder. But those who learn some navigational tips stand a much better chance.

A crisis often causes people to lose objectivity. We've all witnessed such episodes—and experienced them ourselves. Loss of objectivity can occur in the strangest ways and at the oddest times.

Jake and Hal started a business together, investing a great deal of money and time in the venture. For the first few years, things went quite well. But in the fourth year, Hal began demonstrating increasing indifference during meetings. He stopped returning calls to clients and started taking more time off, even during peak seasons. Hal's partner, Jake, watched anxiously as clients became disgruntled and work piled up. Despite numerous confrontations with

Hal, the situation just seemed to get worse. During one confrontation, Hal blew up in anger, telling Jake that their problems were caused by their incompatibility as business partners and by lack of employee productivity.

In desperation, Jake hired a corporate consultant to interview all the employees, thinking that maybe he could get to the bottom of the problem. After a couple of weeks, the consultant stunned Jake with an analysis of the real causes.

Hal's father, grandfather, and great-grandfather had all died of heart attacks when they were age fifty-three. Hal's fifty-third birthday had occurred six months prior to the consultant's interviews. It seems that Hal believed he would die before his fifty-fourth birthday, based on what happened to his forefathers, and this belief had been tainting all of his decisions. In fact, he was so convinced of his impending death that the consultant recommended closing or selling the business before Hal's decisions caused both partners to lose their investment. Hal couldn't deal objectively with the present or the future because of the faulty assumption of his impending death, rooted in his interpretation of the past. Hal and Jake sold the business. Hal is still waiting to die, more than fifteen years later.

To be objective, we must be able to distinguish between present reality and what only exists in our minds. We must be able to approach people and situations without negative bias or prejudice. Prejudice causes us to disregard the truth about people and circumstances, accepting false assumptions that cloud our judgment and inhibit relationship development. Objectivity clears the air, enabling us to see others for who they really are, and helping others see us for who we really are.

Lack of objectivity can also be caused when deeper issues bubble up over insignificant issues. One day in his kitchen, Ken couldn't find the peanut butter. His frustration erupted into a full-blown argument with his wife, Donna. Someone listening to him would have thought he had an especially strong emotional attachment to peanut butter and an obsessive need always to find it in the same place. But to relate to his wife objectively, Ken needed to communicate about the deeper issues, not the insignificant issue of where the peanut butter was. In this case, the deeper issue behind his anger was his tiredness from overwork caused by his compulsion to please others. The argument at hand was useless to Ken or Donna because they were not discussing the real issues. Had he chosen to be vulnerable about his tiredness and struggles at work, Donna might have been able to help by offering her concern and assistance. Instead, he had them stuck in the peanut-butter issue, which left Donna scrambling to defend herself and wondering what Ken could be so upset about.

The same thing happens to leaders at work, in the church, in politics, and everywhere else. Unresolved life issues cause leaders to lose objectivity. When a leader loses objectivity, it can be quite difficult to distinguish organizational problems from the leader's personal problems.

Two Starting Points

There are two basic starting points for regaining objectivity. We can begin with failure or we can begin with truth. The process typically goes faster and requires less pain when we head down the road of receiving and aligning with truth. But because this path requires that we trust God, trust others, and choose vulnerability, many of us end up on the longer, winding, and hazardous road to objectivity. Regaining objectivity is like a fork in the road, where either choice can get you to your destination, if only you can survive the trip! If you refuse to hear and obey the truth, by default you have chosen the road of failure. The key to survival on the more dangerous path is to embrace the lessons failure teaches. When we allow failure to teach us humility, for instance, we discover a shortcut back to the road of truth.

Several years ago, Bruce interviewed a successful medical professional who had been caught in a lie. For years, the woman had been drowning her emotional pain by becoming more and more addicted to drugs. At first, she stole a few pain pills from the medical supply cabinet at work. Then she began raiding the cabinet more often, until finally someone got suspicious and caught her in the act. Only after getting caught did she realize how far she'd gone.

During the interview, Bruce asked her if it would have been helpful to have someone confront her or at least take an interest in her life during that time. She said, "No. I was so convinced I could make certain choices and not suffer. No amount of insight would have helped me." So Bruce asked her what *would* have helped. She answered very quickly and succinctly: "I think I needed a crisis. I needed to lose my practice, almost lose my husband, have my errors made public, and have to acknowledge my wrongs before I finally could see clearly and admit my behavior."

Her words challenged Bruce. Do we all need a crisis to snap us out of our stupor? The medical professional's experience clearly shows that indeed we sometimes have to fail, or at least face impending failure, before we are willing to hear the truth from God and others.

But there is another way.

Turning Back

When the pilot, Jim, was faced with the impenetrable storm, he used all his available navigational tools to overcome it. Then with objectivity, he decided to turn back toward the sun and safety. When leaders face a crisis or a bubbling up of underlying emotional issues, they also can turn back toward safety, but they must make good use of the lower rungs of the character ladder as the navigational tools they need to maintain or regain objectivity. How do they do this?

First, navigators of the fourth rung acknowledge powers far greater than themselves by entrusting themselves to God (rung one). Just as Jim respected the power of the storm and his own inability to fight it, we must have a healthy respect for God and our own limitations in the face of fourth-rung tests. Moving forward recklessly in pride and arrogance may prove fatal to our influence and destiny.

Second, the best navigators are those who, unlike Captain Ahab in Melville's *Moby Dick*, consider the needs of their crew and vessel above their passion to reach a goal. The pilot of Bill's plane could have pressed on and possibly found a way to beat the storm. But would it have been worth risking the lives of his passengers? We should never put those under our care at great risk for the sake of our own selfish pursuits. Remember, our goal on the character ladder is to meet others' needs. Achieving this goal requires a careful consideration of their input by choosing vulnerability (rung two), not just foolhardy pursuit based on our own assumptions.

Third, we must acknowledge that personal testing and risk are unavoidable. The best navigators accept this and prepare as best they can for what's to come. When presented with new circumstances or alternatives, they refuse to deny the truth; instead, they face it and realign their flight plans accordingly (rung three).

Encouraging Words

We cannot promise you that the final rungs will be easy. Learning to pay the price of character-ladder pursuits is quite an adventure. We win some and we lose some. But throughout the process we know that a greater Hand is guiding us—a Hand to which we can entrust ourselves. And we can rest assured that there will be many other hands to help us if we've committed ourselves to the first three rungs.

Let us encourage you with these truths before we move on. First, the God of the Bible can be trusted to stand by and support the humble and help them up the rungs of the character ladder in due time.[9] Second, remember that many others have gone before you and made it. You are not alone in your ascent. Third, if you recall what you've learned along the way, choosing to lean heavily on the lower rungs and finding strength in the relationship and environment rails, you will be able to endure the testing and proving of "paying the price."

Are you ready to put the rails and the first three rungs to the test? Are you ready to count the cost of the fourth rung in order to prepare for your destiny? If not for yourself, would you do it for the benefit of others? For the honor of God? For the sake of love?

Perhaps nowhere is the climb rougher than here. And we feel the limitations of this writing medium keenly. The fourth rung can feel like hell, hurting like a fiery furnace for what seems like an eternity. But such testing removes the dross from our hearts, revealing the purest gold—if we submit to the process.[10]

Jumping off the character ladder can seem so tempting at times, particularly when faced with paying the price. Rather than write about trials and suffering, we would rather pull up a chair, maybe sit by a blazing fire, and just let you talk about your personal fiery furnace. We all need friends who will take a seat and lend an ear.

Short of this, we encourage you to use your imagination. As you read the next few chapters, think of the stories and principles in them as part of a fireside chat with friends. Or perhaps it would be better to imagine them beginning with "Dear friend" and ending with "Sincerely"—letters from long-distance, committed confidants who long for what is best in you to be fully known and appreciated.

Grabbing Hold

- What significant challenges are you facing on the character ladder?
- Who gets your best?
- What do you think hinders leaders from "paying the price"?
- If you were losing your objectivity, how would you reclaim it?

Chapter Nine

Chutes and Leaders

Stories from the Fourth Rung

Character cannot be developed in ease and quiet.
Only through experience of trial and suffering can
the soul be strengthened, ambition inspired, and
success achieved.

—*Helen Keller*

In late 1989 and 1990, financial markets stumbled, and banks and savings and loans failed all over the United States, leaving Circle K Corporation highly leveraged and in serious financial difficulties. The chief executive, Karl Eller, structured a leveraged buyout to solve the crisis. For some reason, however, his plan did not meet the approval of one influential director. The director was so influential, in fact, that Eller soon became estranged from the rest of the board, which forced a difficult fourth-rung decision.

After grappling with his options, Eller determined it would be best for all concerned if he tendered his resignation. Before leaving his position, he structured a workout agreement with Circle K's bankers and creditors in the hopes of keeping the company afloat. But shortly after he left, the agreement hit a snag with one of the banks. Just days later, Circle K declared bankruptcy, leaving Eller, a 20 percent shareholder, with enormous personal losses, no job, and no income. By Eller's own account at the 1997 Entrepreneurs' Forum, Circle K's losses and his own losses had something to do with his own leadership mistakes.[1] All of us cause ourselves some suffering through our own failures, but it's our response to such failures that proves and develops character.

Refusing to Bail Out

Some of Eller's lawyers and bankers urged him to declare personal bankruptcy, but Eller refused. He saw bankruptcy as the easy way out, and his character would not allow him to follow that route: "I committed to pay back what I borrowed, and I knew I had to keep that commitment." Instead of bailing out, he told his bankers the whole truth. He didn't hold anything back. At the Entrepreneurs' Forum, he explained his reasons why: "This follows from integrity, but goes farther into being willing to be transparent, without guile or agenda, to those who place their faith and cash with you." In other words, he chose to be vulnerable with his bankers and aligned with truth by following their plan for debt repayment in humble obedience.

Although some suffering can come as a result of bad choices, suffering and trials can also come from making good choices. Eller had no idea how his decisions would work out. But because he understood the importance of stewarding influence, he committed himself to pay back every cent. It took him three years to settle his debts—a long storm to sail through. Although shaken, he's still standing. Eller recovered from his hard times at Circle K because of the individual decisions of character he had made over the course of his life. He took responsibility for his influence, not just his financial success. Because he paid the price—climbing the fourth rung—his character became the collateral he needed to rise from the ashes. With the help of the people whose trust he had earned, he's once again at the helm of a billion-dollar billboard company that he built from the ground up.

Eller's story reveals a significant reason people of character stick it out through the trials of the fourth rung. (See Figure 9.1.) They don't view their decisions as things they must do to receive a short-term benefit. They choose to do the right thing because the one asset they hold most dear is their influence, something far more valuable than the short-term benefits of the short ladder. Being true

Figure 9.1. The Fruit of the Fourth Rung

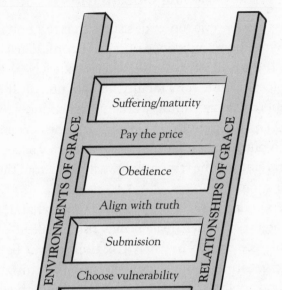

to who they are and who God made them to be develops and tests integrity, and this earns trust, protecting these leaders' right to teach and to love others. They view character maturity as worth the risks of potential setbacks.

Even if nobody else sees or cares about your personal decisions of integrity, God does, and so do you. When Michelangelo painted the Sistine Chapel, people harassed him for the time he took paying attention to details so fine that no one would ever see them from the floor far below. "Who will know?" they asked. "I will," he replied.

Testing Our Mettle

On rung four, leaders encounter decisions that test and retest their mettle, proving their confidence or lack of confidence in the first three rungs. It is a rung of great risk, where leaders bank everything on their choices of trust, vulnerability, and alignment. It is a rung of suffering, where leaders willingly accept and endure pain, loss, or penalty for doing the right thing—embracing the personal costs associated with putting their faith into action. They accept the consequences and steward the responsibilities flowing from their choices on the lower rungs.

As leaders count the cost of the fourth rung, what does "paying the price" put at risk? These leaders may risk privilege—losing the perks they have earned. They may risk their power base—losing the ability to get things done. They may also risk things like title, reputation, and applause. The higher leaders climb, the greater the risks, because their influence has expanded. The greater a leader's influence, the greater the public backlash can be, because the leader has more followers. The stakes have been raised.

In cases like Karl Eller's, leaders may realize the need to step aside, to reconcile parties, to promote others for the greater good, but they will struggle with the potential personal losses accompanying the decision.

Perhaps the greatest risk of the fourth rung comes in the knowledge that we may never get back what we give up. In the refining process, we may sometimes mistakenly cling to the dross as if it were the gold. We may look at wounds from our past, hidden habits in the present, or apparitions about the future as though they define who we are. But it's the gold we're really after: the character and influence we were designed for and that free us to become who God intended us to be. Such freedom always comes at a price, even if we're not the CEO or senior leader.

In their candid book *The Misfortune 500*, Bruce Nash and Allan Zullo expose some of corporate America's most embarrassing moments. What follows here is a chapter by chapter synopsis of what happened to David Edwards and Citicorp as a result of Edwards's attempt to align himself and Citicorp with truth.

A Citicorp Tragicomedy

Chapter 1

Citicorp, the nation's second largest bank holding corporation, is told in 1982 by one of its own officers that the bank's branches in Europe are illegally transferring money to tax-free and tax-reduced accounts in the Bahamas to avoid the tax and currency laws of foreign countries.

Chapter 2

A dispute arises within the Securities and Exchange Commission over Citicorp's improper currency transactions. Some staffers want sanctions against Citicorp. But others say they do "not subscribe to the theory that a company that violates tax and exchange control regulations is a bad corporation." The SEC's chief of enforcement, John Fedders, argues that even if the transactions are illegal, they constitute a "standard business judgment" to try to maximize profits.

Chapter 3

A majority of the five SEC commissioners agree with the novel argument that Citicorp management has no legal duty to disclose the improper transactions, because the firm never represented to stockholders that its top officers possessed "honesty or integrity." The SEC decides to take no action because the case involves banking and taxes, not securities.

Chapter 4

Citicorp officer David Edwards, who first told the bank's senior management of the irregularities, is fired.[2]

We may read this story and laugh at the obvious hypocrisy and shifty reasoning of those involved. But the fact is, climbing the character ladder can seem downright unfair at times. The higher you climb, the more you will be prone to wonder if sticking your neck out for truth, justice, grace, or love is worth the personal suffering that may result.

Chutes and Leaders

On the fourth rung, the leader learns through repeated testing how to weed the bad choices from the good ones, and the good possibilities from the great ones. Situations like those faced by Eller and Edwards represent turning points: they create temptations to play a game of leadership chutes and ladders. Because the fact is that we aren't forced to pay the price—we don't *have* to decide to align with truth. That's quite a temptation! We can escape paying the price simply by sliding on over to the capacity ladder and living a lie, refusing wise counsel and the counsel of our own hearts.

We may convince ourselves that we can still earn perks and privileges from improper pursuits, hoping we can hang on long enough to "make something of ourselves." We may simply capitulate to self-interest, placing the opportunity for personal advancement above the benefit of those we could and should influence through our commitment to integrity.

This temptation has contributed to our current age of golden parachutes, whereby executives enter into a new job with a built-in mechanism to soften their fall from the top. Such parachutes seem quite prophetic, don't they? We wouldn't board a commercial jet if the pilots boarded wearing parachutes, but for some reason we'll work for companies whose executives won't come to work *without* parachutes. How strange.

To be fair, many corporate cultures, with their overemphasis on profit for profit's sake, encourage this counterproductive parachute game. Instead of building communities of grace, they build an atmosphere of "everyone for themselves." Corporations increasingly have abandoned their role as community builders, hoping other social institutions will pick up the slack. Although such parachutes may protect leaders financially, who will protect their influence, relationships, and ultimate destiny? Only when they stay on the character ladder will they be protected in these ways.

Turning points don't just present temptations: they can also create chutes and ladders *opportunities*. When leaders do fall from the capacity ladder (even if they parachute down), they can sometimes more easily slide over to the first rung of the character ladder. The humiliation they experience may be the right remedy for bringing them to the point of acknowledging their need for God and others.

Leaving the Game

Skipping the chutes-and-ladders game altogether represents the best option for leaders. Leaving the game does not mean leaders will escape setbacks. It does mean they must keep a firm grip on the character ladder in order to avoid being consumed by an unhealthy attachment to the capacity ladder alone.

For instance, when former U.S. president Jimmy Carter failed in his bid for a second term, he experienced a profound sense of loss and personal disappointment. Imagine rising to the pinnacle of world political power and then losing it! He faced overwhelmingly low approval ratings at many times during his presidency. A Gallup poll revealed Carter to be one of the few standing presidents whom people did not rank highly as a role model.[3] What does a leader do in such circumstances?

In many cases, leaders turn to what they know best, jumping to tactics they learned on the darker side of the capacity ladder so as to bolster their sense of significance and worth. Attack your opponents, blame others, ditch your friends, and start over on the capacity ladder—anything to prove yourself worthy or right. But

Carter understood some things about the fourth rung of the character ladder that kept him from slipping off.

Trusting God with his future, Carter refused to fire political jabs at his opponent after he lost the election, even after Ronald Reagan got the credit for Carter's work negotiating the release of American hostages in Iran. More than this, Carter spent a great deal of time and effort helping Reagan get up to speed in his new role, making the transition as smooth as possible. Then he quietly disappeared into "private" life after handing over the keys to the Oval Office.

After a few years, it became apparent that Jimmy Carter wasn't through. Through with political office, yes, but his influence began to take a different shape, perhaps more powerful than before. He worked behind the scenes to negotiate world peace, continuing the work he began as president but from an entirely different base of power. He also began building homes for the poor with Habitat for Humanity. His newfound influence flowed from his commitment to selfless service rather than from political power. Some believe his later influence to be far greater and more positive than it ever was during his presidency, which explains why he appears more often and increasingly higher on Gallup's polls of people we look to as our heroes.[4]

The Ways of the Fourth

Carter learned the ways of the fourth rung with a grace many never find. *Paying the price* either tests and proves our character or scares us back into a frantic search for significance on the short ladder. Carter chose to remain with feet firmly planted on the character ladder, passing the tests of the fourth rung.

Reaching our destiny requires such testing. Although we may reach certain goals, we will not reach our destiny without the refining and purifying of our hearts. We need the process of the fourth rung in order to mature. This maturity gives us the strength we need to manage our influence well.

To endure these tests and reach maturity, we must reject the chutes-and-ladders game that tempts us to escape potential setbacks associated with character-ladder choices. We must refuse to cling to the dross and find the gold, looking for the lessons to be learned within our suffering. And there is one more thing we must let go of to keep a firm grip on the fourth rung. We must resist the tendency to expect short-term paybacks in the form of notoriety or praise, because passing fourth-rung tests can actually produce just the opposite.

Mother Teresa chose the stresses of poverty on the streets of Calcutta. She served for forty years before the world took significant notice. William Wilberforce chose an against-all-odds battle against slavery. The bill abolishing slavery wasn't signed until just hours before he died. Abraham Lincoln chose the presidency in the face of civil war. Although he accomplished his goals of reunifying the United States and ending slavery, an assassin's bullet brought the potential benefits of recognition—and his life—to a tragic end.

Amid the potential threats of paying the price, many leaders can easily forget those whom their leadership is intended to benefit: their followers. They may jump off the character ladder in an attempt at self-protection. This is why capacity training alone can never prepare us for the fourth rung. When trained behaviors are distinctly different from who we really are, those behaviors will vanish under crisis, pressure, or competition. Thus we can train a person to save for retirement, but if her desire for instant gratification remains unchecked by character, there will be no check waiting at retirement.

Facing Injustice

The struggles of those who choose to pay the price share many common threads. These leaders ask many of the same questions. Will I satisfy myself or place the needs of others above my own? Will I trust in my own abilities, or will I trust God's trustworthiness? Will I be driven by circumstances or by conviction? Will I demand immediate gratification or accept delays, perhaps even permanent ones?

Questions like these drive home the issue at hand: the fourth rung typically has immediate costs but rarely has immediate benefits. It can sometimes feel unjust or unfair. Yet forfeiting this rung for the sake of short-term gain always leaves our destiny at great risk.

One woman responded well when she encountered unfairness in the form of sexual discrimination back in 1952. In those days, few (if any) firms hired woman attorneys, and they weren't about to change their practices for her, despite her Stanford degree. Her painful circumstances forced a fourth-rung decision early in her career. She suffered from other people's wrong choices and also ultimately from a culture that tolerated and even encouraged such discrimination. In response, she started her own law practice, taking on many cases the other firms wouldn't touch. And this choice led to its own painful trials. But she pressed on in faith.

She had earned a well-deserved reputation for fairness, integrity, and honesty as a lawyer when in 1965 she became assistant attorney general for her state. Four years later, the governor appointed her to a vacated state senate seat, which she then won in the 1972 general election. Soon she was elected as state senate majority leader, the first woman in the United States to hold such a position. Not bad for a woman who was denied a job twenty years earlier. But her first love was law. So she faced another fourth-rung decision. Aligning with the truth about who she was, she chose to let go of political power and switch to the judicial branch of government in 1974, winning a county superior court seat.

By 1978, public figures and political contacts began to urge her to run for governor. She knew that winning such a position would offer the power to positively influence a much larger constituency. Few doubted her abilities or character. She faced another fourth-rung choice.

Privately she discussed her options among a group of advisers. She heard their counsel. She compared it with what she knew about who she was—lessons learned from over twenty years of consistent use of the character ladder. When she emerged from the process, she had made her decision. She would not run.

She had no idea whether she would ever have such an opportunity again. She couldn't have known what would happen next. Too many variables prevented such foreknowledge. She chose not to pursue power, willing to pay the price of letting go of such an opportunity. In this case, she went on to receive far greater influence than she could have hoped for.

Soon a committee appointed her to the state court of appeals. Then, in 1981, President Reagan nominated this woman—Sandra Day O'Connor—to the Supreme Court of the United States. On September 22, 1981, a clear majority confirmed the first woman to serve on the Supreme Court.

We can look at stories like this and assume that fourth-rung choices will lead to such benefits for us. We may view the character ladder as the means to a capacity goal. But this is vanity. Paying the price can never be about winning in the short term—about competing or proving yourself against others. It's about something beyond winning. It's about reaching your destiny by entrusting it to the capable hands of God.

Suffering for Suffering's Sake

We must be careful here. When we encounter times in our lives when paying the price seems confusing and difficult, it helps to remember where we're heading—toward our destiny. Although the fourth rung is no formula for financial prosperity, fame, or power, don't make the mistake of viewing the fourth rung as a choice to suffer intentionally, as if suffering were a formula for reaching your destiny. Destiny cannot be attained by using trials as a point of leverage with God.

Suffering, like integrity, must never be pursued as a virtue. Suffering is a consequence, not a pursuit. As we saw in Karl Eller's case, suffering can come as a consequence of a good decision or a poor one. Or it may simply come as a consequence of living in a fallen world—among humans who treat us inhumanely.

From the ancient ascetic traditions to some of the modern countercultural cults, people have made the mistake of thinking that suffering—because it can challenge the essence of life, meaning, existence, and character—should be pursued on purpose. Such on-purpose suffering has little or no effect on maturity, other than to bring us face to face with our inability to mature by such means. It is interesting that many from these traditions view their self-imposed suffering as a matter of pride—the antithesis of the first rung—yet call their pursuits more spiritual.

Do you recall how the Hebrew Pharisees constantly harassed Jesus for partying so much with "sinners"? People in religious traditions like those of the Pharisees understand the value of ceremony and self-control but *mis*understand the root of such disciplines when they fashion rules as a means to becoming good. The pursuit of goodness or perfection for its own sake never leads to that end. True goodness flows from a fulfilled life and a heart of character. When we experience love, when we mature in character, we are empowered to love others. The roots of pure religion can only be found on the first rung—*trusting God and others with me*. True religion rests upon grace, not upon how good we are at obeying rules.

The roots of false religion can always be exposed by comparing them to the first rung. Any religion that demands performance for acceptance will lead back to the capacity ladder. Thus the Pharisees attempted to make the Jewish people, including Jesus, slaves to their standards of measurement—their custom-designed capacity ladder—complete with a host of "do not taste" and "do not touch" rules. They could not accept grace as an option because they could not fathom a God who would choose to act in love toward the undeserving and "unclean." The capacity ladder, when it stands alone, stands on willpower and self-righteousness. So to give up their claims to spiritual and racial superiority meant the Pharisees would have to let God be God—let the Creator determine the grounds for dispensing acceptance and love. God's grace, as demonstrated by

Jesus, removed the Pharisees' justification for isolating themselves from others whom they preferred to ignore, oppress, or stand over in judgment. Grace always leads to reconciliation, not separatist laws intended to justify bigotry. Self-imposed suffering may look spiritual on the surface. But a good look at its underbelly will reveal overindulgence in pride.

Ascending to the Final Rung

It's not suffering for suffering's sake but rather the choices we make during our suffering that reveal and nurture our character. To pay the price, we must remember that we draw needed strength from God and others, not just ourselves. Paying the price is not about "bucking up" or exercising enough willpower to walk through the flames. It's about finding enough strength in relationships and environments to heed the call—loving God and loving others—according to the Creator's unique design for each of us.

Paying the price means choosing to lead and follow from conviction, rather than reacting to circumstance. It means taking the time to mature, placing a higher value on character than on the short-term benefits of reaching a capacity goal. It means committing to the principles of the long ladder in the context of relationships and environments of grace. As we pay the price, we will learn not to confuse the top of the capacity ladder with the top of the longer ladder. We will accept the consequences of our bad choices, and we will accept the costs of making good choices.

We will pay the price because suffering tests and proves our character. And this character forms the basis for the best kind of influence—the kind that enables us to love, to teach truth, and to create a better world for those all around us. We will pay the price because the fifth rung stands just above us, awaiting those who have been purified and prepared by the hand of God amid the ordinary relationships of their lives.

Are you ready?

Grabbing Hold

- List three to five of your own nonnegotiable values. Does anything prevent you from living according to these values?
- In what relationships has your character been tested?
- In suffering, do you reach for help, or withdraw in isolation?
- What significant life lessons have you learned through suffering?
- Who stands with you in guarding and nurturing your influence and destiny? With whom do you stand?

Chapter Ten

The Fifth Rung

Discovering Your Destiny

None of us knows what the next change is going to
be, what unexpected opportunity is just around the
corner, waiting a few months or a few years to
change all the tenor of our lives.

—*Kathleen Norris*

Henry David Thoreau wrestled with his destiny and purpose as
much as any of us. His growing restlessness and boredom with his
everyday life eventually got the best of him. He decided to escape
to Walden Pond in a personal experiment, the results of which he
published to the world: "I went to the woods because I wished to
live deliberately, to front only the essential facts of life, and see if I
could not learn what it had to teach, and not, when I came to die,
discover that I had not lived."

But, idealistic as it sounds, even this romantic pursuit of life in
the wilderness lost its luster, becoming just as humdrum as his life
in a New England town: "I left the woods for as good a reason as I
went there. Perhaps it seemed to me that I had several more lives to
live, and could not spare any more time for that one. It is remarkable how easily and insensibly we fall into a particular route, and
make a beaten track for ourselves."[1]

Thoreau drew the same conclusions as the ancient King
Solomon, who after pursuing fulfillment to the hilt—in every way
humanly possible—found each pursuit to be nothing but empty
striving, like spitting into the wind.

All of us long for the fifth rung. In our hearts, whether we aspire to large or small dreams, we hope to leave an enduring legacy for our children, our organizations, or even our world. We want to live life as God intended and live it well. We want to find and fulfill our destiny. But what hope do we have? How do we get to the fifth rung?

Discovering Our Destiny

Many have described the characteristics of what we call a fifth-rung leader, and they have drawn similar conclusions. The mystical nature of the fifth rung forms a central theme in their writings.

Peter Senge and Joseph Jaworski refer to synchronicity as a driving force behind fifth-rung leadership. Synchronicity is a state of harmony or congruence, when our lives just seem to fall together for reasons beyond our control. Some call this serendipity or grace. Janet Hagberg describes this mystical quality as power by gestalt, with which leaders lead by wisdom guided by an inner peace. J. Robert Clinton calls it convergence and has demonstrated the pattern in the lives of many biblical leaders, such as Abraham, Joseph, Moses, David, and Daniel. Bob Buford describes fifth-rung folk as sustaining mentors, who exhibit humility, surrender, serenity, and strength.[2]

However the characteristics are described, clearly leaders want to get there—they desire to lead from the fifth rung—to *discover destiny*. But, as we've pointed out in previous chapters, this rung cannot be achieved by superior competency or by an individualistic search for significance. Getting there depends on the process of developing character in the context of the right relationships and environments.

All the other rungs of the character ladder present definitive steps of action. There, leaders make intentional, operative choices. But it's as if leaders are carried to the fifth rung by some unseen force or will beyond their own. They seem to be drawn onto it. Rather than representing an intentional step up from the fourth rung, this fifth step—*discover my destiny*—appears to be more passive, as if it "just happens." But appearances can be deceiving. (See Figure 10.1.)

When Christopher Columbus set out to find a passage to India, he made great preparations for the trip. He had a goal and a plan, and he worked hard to establish the means. In the process he discovered far more than he imagined possible—a whole new world. Discovering destiny can be like this. Leaders make intentional choices on the first four rungs; these choices and their consequences serve as intense preparation for what lies ahead. But when leaders reach the fifth rung, they may be surprised by a destiny far beyond their expectations.

Historical Examples

What do fifth-rung leaders look like? One could choose from many examples, but let's look at two people from back in 1947—a good year for the long ladder—just to get a taste. One was a small, frail woman; the other a tall, impressive man. One expressed overtly religious views; the other held his faith more privately. Yet both possessed tremendous inner strength and a power plainly evident to others. The similarities in their leadership and life purpose and in their development of their inner life are even more striking.

Power Amid Poverty

The first is Mary Teresa Bojaxhiu, who, from the time she was eighteen, knew without a doubt that her life would be different. Twenty years later, in 1947, she founded the Missionaries of Charity and began working with the poorest of the poor in Calcutta. Only after another twenty years of relative obscurity would Mary, known as Mother Teresa, begin to be noticed by outsiders. Her devotion to the poor soon earned her the respect and support of virtually everyone.

Figure 10.1. The Fifth Rung of the Character Ladder

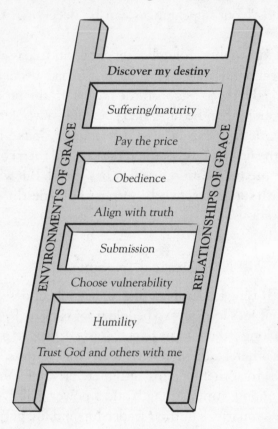

The power of her mission and her person transcended political roadblocks. Equally comfortable asking Ronald Reagan for assistance in feeding Ethiopians as she was soliciting the Marxist-atheist leader of West Bengal, she served God and served the poor, befriending all in this service.

She didn't pursue power, but she certainly received a great deal, through worldwide recognition, audiences with world leaders, honorary doctorates, and even the Nobel Peace Prize. Still, her humility remained evident to all. She would only receive the Nobel award on behalf of the poor, requesting that the award dinner be canceled, which it was, and that the money be used to feed and house the poor and dying.

Before her death, someone called this small, deeply lined, and quiet woman "the most powerful woman in the world." Perhaps she was. But when told of this remark, she responded, "I wish I was. Then I could bring peace to the world."[3] But, back in 1947, this task fell to others, among them a man named George Catlin Marshall.

Marshalling Peace

In 1947, General Marshall began his duties as U.S. secretary of state. Soon thereafter, this man, now "fourth-fifths forgotten" according to his children, somehow pulled off a miracle through what became known as the Marshall Plan.

Marshall had seen firsthand the starving masses in Europe, the fomenting anger of an embattled continent, the seemingly out-of-control breakdown of any sense of order that followed such a horrible war. He took immediate action to rebuild a war-torn world in order to ensure a lasting peace. Putting his reputation and his job on the line in order to protect his president and his peers and to by-pass partisan politics, he made a brief but compelling speech while accepting an honorary doctorate from Harvard.

His speech surprised President Truman, sent shock waves around the world, and galvanized the nation. Did he really believe the nations of Europe could collaborate on such a large scale after two wars as bitter enemies? Could he, unlike Stalin, truly renounce any imperialist aims, especially when Europe was ripe for the picking? Could Marshall really be saying that the most powerful nation on earth would do the opposite—that is, use its power for Europe's protection and seek trust rather than conquest?

In short, yes! Because everyone who knew Marshall understood he was simply extending his own personal beliefs into the arena of foreign policy: set aside the rights of position for the benefit of others, serving them excellently. No matter how powerful you are, share that power with those who view themselves as powerless. The more we examine his life, the more these qualities emerge as paramount to his destiny.

The plan worked, primarily because Marshall assumed the role of a servant leader, working tirelessly to win the support of the American people and Congress on behalf of Europe. Far beyond Marshall's hopes, the Europeans learned to cooperate out of necessity and thus established the framework for the current political structure of the free world, including NATO. Marshall's leadership can be credited with protecting freedom, saving perhaps millions of lives, and rebuilding war-torn countries to take their place in a new, global economy. Like Mother Teresa, he too received the Nobel Peace Prize—the only military person ever to do so.[4]

At the time, many, including Harry Truman and Winston Churchill, believed George Marshall to be the most powerful man in the world. Maybe he was.

Common Ground

Although Marshall and Mother Teresa shared similar goals in 1947—feeding the hungry, working for world peace, and committing their lives to a higher purpose—their positions and organizations could not have been more different. The character ladder works as well for the poor as for the rich, for the politically impoverished as for the politically powerful. We find people of character and thus of tremendous influence from all walks of life. Spiritual power is available to all who climb to the top of the character ladder. So how did Mother Teresa and General Marshall get to the fifth rung?

Their respective paths reveal much about both the short and the long ladder. In fact, these individuals expose an intriguing mystery: they both climbed the short ladder; they both climbed the long ladder.

The choice between the short ladder and the long ladder is not an either-or, black-white decision: it is a both-and decision. Although this may sound contradictory, to climb both ladders represents the only reasonable way to rise to positions of influence with character intact. To reject this duality is to reject reality and growth.

For instance, Marshall climbed the military ranks because he served well, accepting and excelling at increasingly complicated leadership tasks. Mother Teresa had her own short ladder to climb before she could gain permission to embark on her mission. Neither rose to world prominence until late in life—in their sixties—after years of relative obscurity. During their climbs up the short ladder, both endured numerous setbacks and embraced many opportunities for the long-ladder process to take root. So what made the difference in their short-ladder climb?

Extending the Ladders

Both of them integrated the rungs of the capacity ladder with the rungs of the character ladder. They did this by using the correct rails: they found relationships and environments of grace that would honor their capacities while nurturing their character.

Here we make an interesting discovery. When we replace the shaky rails of the shorter ladder with the strong rails of relationships and environments of grace, we can attach them to the rails of the character ladder in a sturdy fashion. Thus, as illustrated in Figure 10.2, the character ladder can function like an extension, leveraging our capacities far beyond what we could have accomplished without character. Ordinary people in ordinary relationships can do extraordinary things with such an integrated ladder.

The lives of Marshall and Mother Teresa confirm that this is so. While ascending the capacity ladder, they made numerous difficult choices—intentional choices—that developed and tested their character in relationships.

As did General Marshall, who, after graduating from the Virginia Military Institute, chose to remain committed and faithful to his first wife, even after she surprised him on their honeymoon night with devastating news: she had a heart condition that would prevent them from ever consummating their marriage.

As did Mother Teresa, who chose to endure the critiques, rejections, and arduous approval process needed to form her new

Figure 10.2. The Integration of the Character and Capacity Ladders

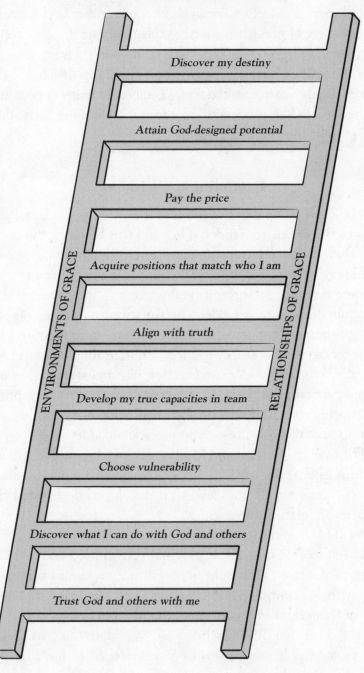

Discover my destiny

Attain God-designed potential

Pay the price

Acquire positions that match who I am

Align with truth

Develop my true capacities in team

Choose vulnerability

Discover what I can do with God and others

Trust God and others with me

ENVIRONMENTS OF GRACE

RELATIONSHIPS OF GRACE

order. She could have struck out on her own, but she instead chose to remain committed to those she trusted.

At the Right Time

How did these people rise to the fifth rung? Neither of them fought, clawed, or manipulated others to get there. In fact, they did just the opposite. For instance, Marshall, amid a political firestorm, chose to remain silent rather than lobby on his own behalf for the chief of staff position. Despite Marshall's inferior rank and Douglas MacArthur's efforts to the contrary, Franklin Roosevelt trusted Marshall implicitly, choosing him anyway, much to the dismay of three senior generals who had vied for the title. Marshall himself tried to talk Roosevelt out of it, concerned that others might have been more qualified according to rank.

Mother Teresa repeatedly turned down opportunities for publicity and personal gain. Still, many leaders visited her and welcomed her counsel, including Princess Diana, who attributed her devotion to humanitarian causes to the influence of Mother Teresa. Beyond this, Mother Teresa's life of self-sacrifice and devotion to the poor stirs something deep within each of us. We see something in her that beckons us to become more than we are. All she longed for was to be the hands and feet of Jesus. Maybe that's what we saw. Maybe that's what causes us to want to be like her in some way. It wasn't her personal power or charisma that drew us in. It was God *in her* that stirred our hearts.

Without a doubt, discovering destiny occurs at just the right time. It can't be forced, and we can't rush it. We typically cannot even imagine it. God takes the initiative to lift us up when he chooses.

The Hebrew-Christian tradition speaks often of this occurrence. In the Psalms we are told, "No one from the east or the west or from the desert can exalt a man. But it is God who judges: He brings one down, he exalts another."[5] Jesus said, "whoever exalts himself will be humbled, and whoever humbles himself will be exalted."[6] And Peter, referring to the Jewish prophets of old, encouraged his followers, "Humble yourselves, therefore, under God's mighty hand, that he may lift you up in due time."[7] As M. Scott Peck wrote in *A World Waiting to Be Born:* "Increasingly, the civil leader or manager begins to sense that the power of her position is not hers. It is not her possession; it is not hers to possess. The power belongs to God, and the proper role of the civil leader is merely to be a conduit and to steward that power as God's agent. Merely! What a paradox! To exercise temporal power with civility is to undertake a role of great glory, and it can only be undertaken with genuine humility."[8]

When we examine the natural talents of great influencers we often find little that distinguishes them from others. But when we look at their character, we find the essential ingredients of their greatness. They trusted God and others. They chose vulnerability. They aligned with truth and paid the price for their decisions. God then elevated these prepared people to positions of honor and influence beyond their potential apart from the character ladder.

Thus, Mother Teresa could turn down the Nobel award dinner in her honor for the sake of the poor. And G. C. Marshall could strengthen war-torn countries by offering grace and encouraging community. God places people he can trust into the right places at the right time. He tests and refines them on the character ladder so that when the right opportunities arise, they are ready for the challenge.

The reciprocal is also true. Those who refuse any rung or rail of the character ladder not only will be ill prepared to discover their destiny but also may miss it altogether. Discovering destiny depends on God giving us the eyes to find it. There is a mystery to it. But this does nothing to minimize our own responsibility to seek and evaluate the opportunities presented to us. There is no greater loss than to come to that purpose in life for which we were born and to not be prepared.

Don't Plan It, But Don't Miss It

Getting to and staying on the fifth rung has nothing to do with pursuing power. It is about learning how to receive power. We cannot plan it. In fact, we shouldn't even try to plan it. But we certainly don't want to miss it either. Therefore, we must prepare for it.

Can you imagine what our world would look like under the influence of fifth-rung leaders? Maybe that's too utopian—but maybe not. Didn't Jesus teach us to pray, "Your kingdom come, your will be done, on earth as it is in heaven"?[9] Praying for God's will to be done on earth—praying for earth to look more like the kingdom of heaven—that's a prayer with far-reaching implications! Can we at least begin to envision such leadership in our own families, churches, businesses, and government?

The fifth rung is no panacea. It does not cure all our ills or pave the way to a utopian life. It is rooted in reality. It is dependent on the first four rungs and the rails of the character ladder. But in the climb we find peace. We find joy. We find fulfillment. We find God, and we find a community that helps us know our Creator and ourselves more fully.

Thoreau was right to sacrifice so much in his search for fulfillment of his inner longings. But he went down the wrong path and found it well worn. At least he was honest enough to admit it!

Can we admit it? Can we let go of our well-worn paths and follow the one less traveled? Can we ascend the ladder of character to discover our destiny? Discovering destiny is far from passive. In fact, it may be the most active rung of all. The fifth rung presents us with at least seven significant challenges. If we don't welcome these challenges, our refusal will keep us from discovering our destiny. Those who have made it to the fifth rung risk slipping off if they forget to actively greet these challenges. They may finish their lives poorly, losing the influence they have gained. We'll look at the seven fifth-rung challenges in the next chapter.

Grabbing Hold

- Are you in a process that is helping you discover your destiny? If not, what steps are necessary to enter that process?
- Do you value servant leadership?

- What part do you think God plays in shaping your destiny?
- Which ladder best describes your ascent? What are the potential outcomes of your choices?
- Do you know anyone who has integrated the two ladders well?

Chapter Eleven

Keeping Your Balance

Seven Challenges of the Fifth Rung

A hundred times every day I remind myself that my
inner and outer life depend on the labors of other
men, living and dead, and that I must exert myself
in order to give in the same measure as I have
received and am still receiving.

—*Albert Einstein*

"Everyone has a built-in 'risk index' that's somewhere between 0
and 1.0," Herman Cain, CEO of Godfather's Pizza, told the 1997
annual conference of the League of Nebraska Municipalities. "Only
you can determine how much risk you're willing to take—not only
in your job, but also in your daily life. If your risk index is 0, you're
afraid to get out of bed in the morning for fear there might not be a
floor there. But if your risk index is 1.0, you'll jump out of an air-
plane without a parachute, knowing you're going to find one before
you hit the ground! There aren't too many people with a risk index
of 1.0, but good leaders need risk indexes that are 'north of 0.5.'"

Leaders who aspire to the fifth rung must continue to take risks,
because taking risks identifies and develops fifth-rung leadership.
This tough challenge just keeps getting tougher as the years roll by.

The older we get, the less elasticity we have. Not just our physical health, but our emotional and financial health can't bounce
back as quickly as when we were younger. It becomes harder and
takes longer to handle flawed choices and circumstances. We naturally develop patterns and rhythms throughout our lives. This is a
healthy thing. But the more ingrained these patterns and rhythms

become, the less tolerance we have for disturbing them. So we may tend to avoid taking the kinds of chances we would have risked when we were younger.

Therefore, the first challenge of the fifth rung involves a commitment to confront complacency. Leaders must avoid overdependence on patterns of safety and security that can lead to indifference, smugness, and loss of creative energy. This means fifth-rung leaders will always put themselves at risk of some kind of discomfort or insecurity. They will actually strive to increase their risk index as they age, rather than decrease it.

When leaders have been on the fourth rung, typically for many years, they understand the temptations and struggles of increased responsibility. By the time they are ready to discover their destiny, they know from personal experience what it means to pay the price. They weigh the costs of pursuing goals—especially lofty ones—very carefully.

A younger, less-tested leader may jump headlong into the pursuit of a wonderful goal. But if she doesn't have the necessary character maturity, her attempt may lead to discouragement, or even bitterness. Thankfully, the young typically have far more energy and elasticity to bounce back from their failures. But the mature realize what it really takes to accomplish something significant and are more careful with their investments of time and energy.

The benefits of age and experience should make leaders less foolhardy, but not to the extent of their becoming overly self-protective. Sitting back and resting on their laurels can keep leaders off, or knock them off, the fifth rung fast. Janet Hagberg makes this very clear:

> One thing I know for sure: You cannot become a leader in the sense I describe without being keenly aware of yourself and willing to give up many of the traditional beliefs about power and leadership. You must at some point take a "leap of faith" toward the emerging model of what it means to truly lead and away from the need to be successful, famous, rich, in control, or powerful. The kind of leadership I am

advocating arises out of the understanding of pain, the loss of inno-
cence, the love of others, the larger purpose, the pursuit of wisdom,
the honor of life. Ask yourself if you are willing to take the risk.[1]

There are no guarantees except one. When we choose to climb
up the character ladder, we will extend beyond our own individual
potential and self-protective isolation. On the other hand (writes
Max De Pree), "by avoiding risk, we really risk what's most important in life—reaching toward growth, our potential, and a true contribution to the common good."[2] The fifth rung transports us into
the realm of the common good—the realm of grace. We will become leaders who serve others—who act as stewards rather than
slaves of influence. This only comes when we believe, deep in our
hearts, that ultimately all influence comes from the hand of God for
the purpose of benefiting others.

In so believing, fifth-rung leaders may shun the race to be king
of the hill even though, paradoxically, they would make the best of
kings. They will also avoid becoming the fool on the hill—alone,
ashamed, and teetering on the edge of disaster—and instead make
decisions based on their convictions. They will, in fact, become ser-
vants on the hill, setting aside their rights and power for the benefit of those they influence. For fifth-rung leaders, leadership becomes
stewardship.

Knock, and the Door Will Be Opened

This stewardship brings leaders to the second challenge of the fifth
rung. Despite contentment with their own present circumstances,
they must express both compassion and conviction by actively
seeking new opportunities to do so. For fifth-rung leaders, this usually involves an ever-expanding search for ways to care for and improve the circumstances of others.

It can be difficult to keep mining for such opportunities without
experiencing a cave-in. Leaders may become victims of their search
for a couple of reasons. First, because opportunities usually increase
in direct proportion to leaders' influence, fifth-rung leaders may

experience opportunity overload. Some leaders receive hundreds of requests for help each week! In overreaction, leaders may arbitrarily shut out great possibilities. Second, seeking new opportunities can cause a gradual loosening of a leader's grip from the first four rungs as occasions to seek personal gain *above* positive influence become more frequent. Instead, leaders should keep alert for the *right* opportunities. How can they tell the difference when encountering a number of options?

Fifth-rung opportunities are those in which we can serve others on the basis of our compassion and convictions. Wherever we are on the "influence scale" matters less than making sure we arrive without jeopardizing our followers or our own souls. There is a story of a man who gave up everything to seek God in the desert with a band of hermits. His fellow hermits sent him to town to sell a couple of old donkeys, but he refused to tell potential buyers anything but the truth—that the donkeys were old, stubborn, and rather worthless animals. When he returned with the donkeys still in tow, his fellow hermits demanded to know why. He replied, "Do you imagine for a moment that I left home and gave everything away, all my camels and cattle and sheep and goats, in order to make a liar of myself for the sake of two old donkeys?"[3] We should all be as careful to avoid sacrificing our convictions for the sake of a goal. Further, we should actively seek out opportunities to express such convictions.

Back in the early 1990s, the chaplain of the U.S. Senate, Richard Halverson, tendered his resignation with the promise to remain in office until a successor was found. The search for a new chaplain was accelerated when Senator Bob Dole became majority leader and asked Senator Mark Hatfield to chair a bipartisan committee and come up with a candidate to be presented for election by the Senate. Two hundred and six candidates were reviewed, and a short list was developed.

Senator Hatfield had thought of Lloyd Ogilvie for the job but assumed that he would not be ready to leave his position as senior pastor of the First Presbyterian Church of Hollywood and his national television and radio ministry.

Meanwhile Ogilvie kept secret his vision of many years to someday be Senate Chaplain. He had known and admired Richard Halverson for thirty years and had revered the memory of some of the distinguished former chaplains like Peter Marshall.

Then one day, a friend who knew Ogilvie's heart called Senator Hatfield to tell him that, if considered, Dr. Ogilvie might be open. The result was a series of phone conversations between Hatfield and Ogilvie. When friends heard of the possibility, recommendations were sent to Senators Hatfield and Dole and the committee. Ogilvie was placed on a short list of six finalists. Eventually he became the unanimous choice of the committee and was elected the sixty-first chaplain on January 24, 1995.

Lloyd and his wife, Mary Jane, knew God had called them to Washington. Good thing, because they were able to face the challenges of a move away from children and grandchildren, a great congregation, and a nationwide media ministry. But God guided and provided. He was the author and enabler of the dream, and He helped the Ogilvies through a challenging first year that included a life-threatening illness for Mary Jane. God was faithful and used even this crisis to bond the Ogilvies to the Senate family.

Dr. Ogilvie accepted the position, not for the prestige but for the opportunity to speak into the personal lives and families of those who influence an entire nation. He has since touched the lives of countless people, from heads of state to staff to custodians. God gave him the vision and then gave him the desires of his heart. Now, in Bible studies for senators, senators' spouses, and Senate staff, lives are being changed and authentic renewal is taking place.

Like Ogilvie, we all should actively seek out ways to benefit others through our convictions and compassion. In other words, we must continually seek to find ways to *integrate* our hearts with our hands, our agenda with our dreams, and our capacities with our character. Otherwise we put our destiny at risk.

Teachable Teachers

Challenge number three stems from two parallel demands: leaders must continue to change and grow; and fifth-rungers typically are sought out as mentors by others who want to change and grow. Because leaders must change and grow, and because they are sought out as mentors, interdependency becomes even more important on the fifth rung. Change and growth require teachability. To remain teachable, leaders can let go of their pride and let the other ordinary people around them provide input into their lives and decisions. Interdependency goes the other way too. In addition to remaining teachable, leaders are also sought out to teach. As a leader, you can remain available to mentor others. This means you may get less done in the present, but you will actually accomplish far more in the future by pouring your life into the people who can carry on those things that are nearest and dearest to your heart. The willingness to remain teachable and to be taught stems from the commitment to interdependency, a character trait developed on the first four rungs of the character ladder. Welcoming this challenge helps fifth-rung leaders avoid the ever-present dangers of isolation and stagnation that can cause them to slip from the character ladder.

One of the first signs of an endangered leader is a decrease in his willingness to hear and learn from the experiences of others. Beware of this trap! Remember, fifth-rung experiences come from God, not your own superior abilities or character. Protection and direction come from listening, hearing, and aligning with the truth others have to tell us.

As you learn from others, record what you are learning. There are two reasons for this. First, you will find that as you write things down, you gain clarity. Second, perhaps you will be able to use what you have recorded for someone else's benefit. After all, community is a two-way street, and again, fifth-rung leaders are often sought out as coaches and guides for others.

Although serendipity and synchronicity may seem commonplace to you if you're a fifth-runger, recognize that these same experiences come to those on the other rungs. God often allows leaders at other stages to experience tastes of grace in order to give them a vision of what could be, as well as to test their stewardship of that experience.

Many have heard of Joni Eareckson, the woman who rose to international influence as an artist and public speaker after losing the use of all her limbs. But few ever heard of Steve Estes, who had led Eareckson out of her depression amid the pain of facing a future in a wheelchair. After Eareckson had written her first best-selling book, she asked Steve to help her with her second. At the time, Steve was a twenty-something youth leader, and Ken was a high school kid under his influence.

Ken remembers visiting a special event at a bookstore with Steve. Steve was not the focus of the event, but when Ken handed a copy of Steve's newly published book to the store owner and whispered that the coauthor was in the store at that very moment, Steve suddenly found himself in the spotlight. Ken naively thought Steve would thank him, but Steve gave him one of those looks that could kill as he very reluctantly received the microphone. Steve used the opportunity to praise Joni's work for a few seconds and then tried to disappear again into the crowd.

Afterward Ken asked Steve why he was upset with what he had done. Steve replied that he viewed his work with Joni as a privilege God had granted him, not a means to score popularity points. Steve recognized the fortuity of his friendship with Joni, but he never wanted to use that experience for the wrong reasons. Steve realized that his early fifth-rung experiences did not qualify him as a fifth-rung leader. They were tests, not a reward to be leveraged. And he didn't want to use God's gift to benefit his own ego or detract from Joni's influence.

Steve's advice helped Ken. And Steve's passing those tests, when people like Ken tried to force him into improper roles, paved the way for Steve's maturity and later influence. Ken's time under

Steve's influence was brief—a few short years—but Steve's influence in his life has had an impact on many of Ken's choices for over twenty years.

Setting aside the time it takes to affirm and encourage others to walk the path you have walked may leave less time for other seemingly urgent matters, but it is a task that fifth-rung leaders must accept. To draw a mentoree's attention to her own fifth-rung experiences; to help her see the work of God in her life; to join you in the climb up the character ladder—these are the things that make a huge difference in the lives of those whom leaders influence.

Henrietta Mears made a habit of discerning and affirming the early fifth-rung experiences of those in their teens and twenties. J. Robert Clinton says, "she had an uncanny ability . . . for spotting potential leaders early on."[4] The awesome power of this practice is demonstrated in the lives of those she influenced: Richard Halverson, former chaplain of the Senate; Bill Bright, one the most influential voices on the nation's college campuses during the twentieth century; along with others, including the Rev. Billy Graham.

Perhaps this process could be built into all kinds of organizations. Maybe you could hire a director of leadership development or integrate character-ladder principles into your current training process. Maybe you could start with your spouse or children.

Bill and Bruce have at different times taught leadership classes in which they encouraged developing leaders to create a time line of key events and decisions in their lives. It helps emerging leaders tremendously as they find answers about their tomorrows by seeing the hand of God in their yesterdays.

Hear and be heard. Teach and be taught. Remain teachable and teach others along the way. Remember, the only difference between a rut and a grave is the length.

Don't Dare to Compare

The fourth challenge is pivotal for fifth-rung leaders. Instead of constantly measuring themselves against some standard of arrival, they must place their destiny fully into the hands of God. Very practically, to ensure their destiny is in the right hands, they must refuse to measure it by comparing their sphere of influence to that of others.

"Well," you might say, "then how can we know if we have reached the fifth rung?" Here lies the dilemma. We can't tell by power or position, because these can be deceptive.

We know a retired high school history teacher who leads from the fifth rung. Chuck is in his seventies now, and he sometimes falls asleep in church and sneaks cookies when his very concerned and disciplined wife isn't looking. But the man exudes peace, contentment, and grace. Hang out with Chuck for five minutes and you can't help but be encouraged. He doesn't even have to say anything. Yet his influence is penetrating. Many speak of the difference this unassuming man has made in their lives.

You probably won't get a chance to meet Chuck before his days on earth are through. But if you did, you would probably wonder how such a man, who seems so imperfect and, well, normal, can exude such strength, honesty, and vulnerability. The answer is that he has discovered his destiny, receiving it from the hand of God.

No. We can't tell a fifth-runger solely by breadth of influence or height of position. This is how we know: in positions of influence, however great or small, they retain a character-ladder perspective on life. They will not pursue their potential at the expense of conviction and character. They will look to God and their community—not their own evaluation—to affirm their influence. They seldom rely on short-ladder power or lapse into its tactics. They care less about magnitude and more about making right choices on the lower rungs. This keeps power from corrupting and absolute power from corrupting absolutely.

It's not that fifth-rung leaders don't respect positions of power. Far from it! They honor those in positions of authority because they understand the nature of such influence. In fact, they might actually hold such positions.

After serving eight years in the House of Representatives, Dan Coats filled the Senate seat vacated when Dan Quayle became vice president of the United States. After winning a special election to serve the remainder of Quayle's term, Coats was elected to serve a full six-year term in 1992. He understood the nature of political power and influence and made good use of it. But in 1998, Coats decided not to run for a second full term. Why?

During his life and tenure in government, Coats developed some strong convictions. He learned something about how the most profound changes occur in a life, a community, and a culture: that the most fundamental issues can only be addressed in relationships—one-on-one encounters in which one life deeply touches another. Because he ardently believes in the positive, life-transforming changes that can occur through mentoring young people, he set aside the prestige and power of national government and now serves as national board president of the Big Brothers and Big Sisters organization.

If he had made his decision by comparing political power, he probably would not have chosen the Big Brothers role. But he made his decision based on convictions that were rooted deep in his understanding of who he was. Fifth-rung leaders must avoid the danger of comparing their influence to others—not devaluing roles of influence but recognizing that some values transcend the bottom lines of power or wealth. They must live for the affirmation of God instead.

Sharing the Rewards

Often leaders can do very well in the midst of a team or community, rising to the fifth rung, only to make the mistake of moving forward without those who brought them there.

No leader rises to the fifth rung in isolation. Yet they may decide to exact an exclusively personal benefit from the sacrifices and influence others have invested into them. For instance, pastors may teach and be taught within an intimate community or leadership team for years and then succumb to the deception that they can capitalize on their team's success without sharing the rewards.

Granted, communities often don't know how to recognize or honor a leader's maturity. So when honor comes, often through activities and opportunities outside their immediate community, leaders may set up some way of personally profiting from their experiences, forgetting to honor their community for its role in their life.

The same situation occurs in companies and corporations when senior leaders impose burdensome performance requirements on their employees but then disproportionately reward themselves for the results.

So, what is the fifth challenge? Fifth-rung leaders choose to benefit *with* their team and community, rather than just benefiting *from* them.

Three people recently developed and marketed a product. Each of the three contributed commensurate hours and talents to the project, assuming they would benefit together in its success. But when the time came to sell the company, one of them pocketed several million dollars, whereas the other two simply lost their jobs.

In contrast, one innovative Silicon Valley firm pays all employees equitably (not equally) based on their years with the company, job responsibility, and other factors. When the company makes a profit, everyone benefits equitably. Even janitors can make a huge bonus. How do you think this affects productivity? Other excellent companies and organizations follow similar policies, but they are still a minority.

In *The Music of Silence*, David Steindl-Rast describes how the monks under St. Benedict's rule were encouraged to include others in their blessings. As the servers brought food to the dinner table, the monks would never ask for anything they needed, but instead look out for what their neighbor needed. This practice led to a famous story that Steindl-Rast recounts: "A monk . . . notices as he's eating his soup that a mouse has dropped into his bowl. What is he to do? He's to pay attention to his neighbor's needs, not his own. So he helps himself by calling the server and pointing out, 'My neighbor hasn't got a mouse.'"[5] Leaders who look out for the interests of others stand a much better chance of staying on the fifth rung.

Fluidity and the Right Relationships

The sixth challenge has to do with the interplay of time, priorities, and relationships. Early in leaders' development, they learn how to manage their time according to priorities. They may be told to schedule so many hours for this priority and so many hours for another. The question that demands an answer is, What priority do I commit the most time to?

Life has so many dimensions: social, familial, intellectual, spiritual, vocational, emotional, and physical. How do we prioritize these? Or even balance them all? As life becomes more complicated, things rarely work in a compartmentalized fashion. The danger in trying to balance or prioritize compartments is that sometimes leaders can give themselves permission to violate key relationships in the process.

A corporate climber may sacrifice marriage and family in order to reach the goal of a vice presidency or a six-figure income. A parent—whether a magnate or a missionary—may abandon his or her children in a variety of ways, solely for the sake of a cause. And the pendulum can swing back the other way. Some now shirk very reasonable job responsibilities, playing their family values as a trump card in order to win special rights or justify poor performance.

Does putting spirituality first mean we exclude our family health or vocational excellence or physical needs? And isn't caring for our family a social activity? And isn't our vocation a spiritual activity? And aren't our finances an emotional activity? The healthier and more mature we get, the more difficult it becomes to arbitrarily pull life apart into separate pieces.

It is when life gets the craziest and most chaotic that fifth-rung leaders can shine, because they have learned to be fluid, rather than insist on strict, compartmentalized priorities. They lead by principle, honoring the right relationships at the right time, moving from one need to the other with relative ease (most of the time anyway). Those who lead by rules and regulations may put God at the top of the priority list and give themselves permission to violate others, which of course dishonors God. Those who lead by principle may actually seem to thrive on chaos and ambiguity, but they rarely contribute to the chaos by hurting others, and they seldom exhibit ambiguity in their relational commitments. Those who aspire to remain on the fifth-rung must be cautious with fluidity, because the press of commitments may tempt them to acquiesce into the comfort of a few familiar relationships, trading off others. We must not mistake fluidity to mean we have permission to delete discomfort from our schedules.

When Bruce attended postgraduate school, he observed the fifth-rung characteristics of the school's well-respected president. While overseeing a rapidly growing institution, this top administrator also demonstrated uncommon devotion to his wife, who suffered from a long-term illness and was often bedridden. The president honored his promises to both his wife and his job with exceptional fluidity. Neither felt neglected or dishonored. In fact, just the opposite was true.

The president's administrative assistant of twenty years said, "He honored both commitments with grace and ease. They were both at the top of his agenda. For example, we would never schedule two back-to-back weekends away, and for several years we scheduled his time at the school for Monday through Wednesday, with the balance of his administrative duties conducted from his home office. Yet the institution never suffered from an absence— he was continuously available from anywhere in the world. You never knew any pressure that he was under, and both the family and the school were substantial beneficiaries. His actions followed a plan of priority that stemmed from his values to honor God in *all* his relationships."

If you knew this president, you probably never would have heard him share how he would alter his schedule to lovingly care for his wife. And you would not have noticed the changes due to his commendable success in running the school. He was a fifth-rung leader choosing to assume the challenge of giving the right attention to the right relationships at the right times.

Resolving to Resolve

There is one more challenge all fifth-rung aspirants must accept. People who go through good management training are taught to develop their strengths and delegate their weaknesses. Good advice. But in fifth-rung training, we must actively do something else. We must continuously work to resolve our character weaknesses—to work through our unresolved issues—rather than just wink at them or hope we can manage them away.

No matter how much one matures, character weaknesses and unresolved issues will still surface throughout one's life. It's as if our hearts are like a dark room with a shaded window. Early in life, God only allows the window shade to go up a little, letting in small streams of light to reveal things that must be dealt with on our way up the character ladder. As we mature, God raises the window shade a bit further, based on what we can handle amid our current environment and relationships. At no point does God throw up the shade completely. We couldn't handle that. We shouldn't even try to handle everything at once. But to remain on the fifth rung, we must continue to risk resolving the issues God does allow us to see, even though this can cause emotional pain and relational stress.

We do this in the context of a culture of grace, where relationships and environment converge to create the safety and acceptance we need to address the issues of our hearts. When fifth-rungers commit themselves to this process, they often seem to be in a more fragile place than at other times in their lives. They may appear more dependent than they need to, because they recognize the necessity of interdependence in the accomplishment of anything significant.

Interdependence is the hallmark of a fifth-rung leader. He can always be found in a community where he is loved and, in return, pours out his life in service to others. If you want to know whether you are a fifth-rung leader, it is to your community you must turn. Personal intuition or running away to a desert has little value in this matter. Instead, ask your friends. Ask your community. They'll tell you, if you let them. In fact, this is the truest test of discovering destiny—when those you influence acknowledge God's hand in elevating you, despite their knowledge of your weaknesses.

The litmus test of community feedback signals whether leaders are accepting or avoiding the challenge of resolving the issues still lurking within their hearts. When leaders commit themselves to trust, vulnerability, and alignment with truth, even after they've reached the fifth rung, the resulting interdependence and health protects them from inner flaws that could cause a fall. Dealing with unresolved issues in community also shatters the dangerous myth of arrival—an insidious inducement to disaster by which we think we have nothing more to gain from the input of others.

Emerging or maturing leaders who succumb to the myth of arrival may be tempted to force the fifth rung. This usually occurs when leaders lack environments or relationships of grace, which encourages them to hide or avoid the truth about their weaknesses and character flaws. But it can also occur when leaders compare their flaws to the flaws of those on the lower rungs and wrongfully assume they can just sweep their own weaknesses under a rug. A leader who has an early fifth-rung experience and interprets it to mean early arrival at the top can also be sucked into the myth of arrival.

When leaders ignore their own issues outside a community of grace, they may be bewitched into manufacturing a premature message of convergence or arrival in order to legitimize their leadership. To followers, these leaders can often look like fifth-rung leaders. Leaders like Jim Jones, David Koresh, and other cultists and mass murderers demonstrate how catastrophic the results can be. Most of the time, the cases are much less severe, but they all stem from a myth, perpetuated by refusal to resolve the issues of the heart in the context of community.

Bill once heard a young woman describe her sense of arrival— her own fifth-rung convergence experience. Listing a series of accomplishments and relationships, she described a clear path of ascendancy that she believed spoke to God's preparation of her life for a particular vocation and far-reaching influence. It sounded quite logical and probable that her next occupation would take her to a place of significant influence in the world. But she was sorely disappointed. She failed in her new endeavor. It turned out to be another fourth-rung lesson in patience and perseverance. She had set herself up for a fall that shattered her. Unmet expectations left her bitter and angry at the world and at God.

Just because we are on the fourth rung does not mean our next opportunity will be our destiny. If we make the mistake of misreading our place on the ladder, we get trapped into evaluating our next steps in terms of the perceived increase of influence in each successive opportunity. The fifth rung just doesn't work this way.

Fifth-Rung Realities

You cannot plan your destiny. But you can prepare for it. To discover your destiny and remain on the fifth rung, you cannot avoid the seven challenges by manufacturing your own version of paradise, safe and secure from potential danger. Rather, you first must confront complacency, avoiding patterns that may lead to indifference or hubris. Second, seek out new ways to express your compassion and convictions—to serve others from your heart. Third, remain teachable and make yourself available to teach others. Fourth, instead of comparing your influence to others', place your future fully into the hands of God, seeking a destiny of faith over a destiny described by sight alone. Fifth, share the benefits of your influence with those around you, rather than benefit at their expense. Sixth, approach your relationships and priorities in a fluid way instead of scheduling your life to the point of excluding relationships that really matter. Finally, aggressively seek to resolve your own character issues and weaknesses, continuing to trust others with your vulnerability and to align with the truth, even when it exacts a high price.

Each of the seven challenges has inherent costs. Each also possesses potential rewards. Challenge can imply great danger, but great gain as well. Embracing these seven challenges to remain on the fifth rung will bring you closer to extraordinary influence—the kind that provides the greatest contributions to the common good. Are not these leaders—the kind that bless the world by their gracious presence—the kind of leaders you want to follow? Are not these the kind of leaders we want to become ourselves? The seven challenges may seem scary to some, but for most, the possibility of leaving a legacy characterized by compassion, selflessness, integrity, and concern will far outweigh their fears. Indeed, the hope of our world hangs in the balance, as we anticipate leaders who will weigh the costs and rewards and find the scales tipping in favor of climbing the character ladder.

Grabbing Hold

- Which of the seven challenges have you encountered? Which have you refused to accept?

- For you, is discovering your destiny worth the risks? If not, where is the disconnect?

- What challenges are you accepting for the benefit of those you are influencing?

- In what relationships, and on which team, are you benefiting "with" rather than "from"?

- How have you benefited from another person's fifth-rung experiences?

Chapter Twelve

Becoming the Kind of Person
Others Want to Follow

Let them remember there is meaning beyond
absurdity. Let them be sure that every little deed
counts, that every word has power, and that we
can—every one—do our share to redeem the world
in spite of all absurdities and all frustrations and all
disappointments. And above all, remember that the
meaning of life is to build a life as if it were a work
of art.
—*Rabbi Abraham Heschel (quoted in Greenleaf, 1977)*

A single work of art can affect many different people in many different ways. Sometimes we stand before a painting as though we were standing before a mirror. We may see something of ourselves reflected in the swirls, daubs, and commingled colors. Sometimes a painting can act like a window. Instead of looking *at* it, we see *through* the canvas into the mind and heart of the artist. Perhaps we even see something more, something we may have longed to see, just beyond the surface, awakening us to something deeper. Sometimes we may even see glimpses of God.

Ken once learned something while viewing a painting by Chattanooga artist Ed Kellogg. From up close, the painting appeared to be random splatters of paint in colors that didn't make any sense. But from about four feet away, the random strokes and splashes fell together into recognizable, realistic images. From six feet away, the images began to speak to Ken's heart, because Ken saw something more than the human artist's intent. The canvas became a window, revealing a viewpoint that has stuck with Ken for years: though life may appear random, even ugly from up close, if you have the right perspective and distance, you can see beauty. Compelling beauty. Breathtaking beauty. Even though the subject matter is common enough—ordinary people living ordinary lives—the hand of a Master is at work.

Each life is a work of art, created with living, breathing paints with a will of their own. We actively participate in the process of our own making. We sometimes get glimpses into the Master's purpose as we see the brush strokes in our lives come together. But from day to day, it can be difficult to make sense of the seeming absurdities of our own foibles and troubles. We may question the Creator's choice of colors, technique, or materials. Some of us may even question whether God's hand is in it at all, though we long for it to be so. As Bill once wondered about his own life: "Did God do any of this, or has it just been me all along?"

More Than What I Can Make of Myself

Alone at home, trying to sleep in ninety-five-degree heat with no air conditioning, Bill sensed the question stalking him like a hungry pit bull. He had expressed faith in God for over fifteen years. Yet as he looked back at his life, he observed little evidence that anything supernatural had influenced the outcome. Thinking of his job, his family, and his church activities, Bill wondered, "Can any of this really be attributed to anything but my own efforts?"

Bill had been looking for the evidence of God's hand in the external things—career, ministry, and family success. Then it dawned on him: "This isn't about what has been done. It's about me, isn't it? Could God be asking me to trust him with my weaknesses? My destructive habits? The things I don't let others see? Could God possibly turn *me* into something good? I know I can't turn me around. Maybe God can."

Bill had tried over and over again to overcome the wounds of his past and his own self-inflicted pain, but he could not get past them. Each time a significant opportunity arose in his life, these were the things that kept Bill down and held him back. They kept him from emotional intimacy with his wife. They created a gap between Bill and his kids. They hurt his job performance and career choices. They even distanced Bill from those he longed to reach out to, the hippies and street kids of the early 1970s.

That night marked a turning point. Bill asked God to turn his life into far more than he could make it on his own, by dealing with the issues of his heart that affected his character and influence.

Two years later, Bill flew to Los Angeles to meet with the managing partner of the accounting firm he worked for. Over lunch, this very distinguished gentleman presented Bill with the opportunity to begin the process of becoming a partner in the firm. Bill truly appreciated the offer but said he and his wife could not decide until January, three months later. Thinking Bill was fishing for a better offer, the managing partner became somewhat irritated. When Bill assured him otherwise, the partner canceled his afternoon appointments. He spent the rest of the afternoon trying to find out what in the world could be so important that Bill might walk away from such an opportunity. They had a great discussion, but that's another story.

The following Monday, a political friend called Bill from Washington. "Barry Goldwater is here with me. We'd like to ask you something. Would you be willing to come to Washington to work as part of the Arizona delegation of the Republican Party?"

Again, Bill answered, "Thank you. This sounds like an incredible opportunity, and I'm honored by the request, but I can't let you know until January. My wife and I . . ."

"What?" the friend responded. "Bill, I know you're interested in politics. Do you realize what this could lead to?"

Bill could hear Goldwater saying some choice words in the background. Neither his friend nor Goldwater took Bill's response very well: "As I was saying, Grace and I are trying to decide what we should pursue during the next season of our lives. I'm not ruling it out. I'm just saying I need until January."

The following Tuesday, the president of Bill's alma mater called. "Would you consider coming back here in a significant leadership role? We'd really like you to consider it."

Bill responded the same way.

Three weeks. Three opportunities. Which should he pursue? Accounting? Politics? Education? All appealed to Bill strongly. All offered a significant leadership role. All possessed inherent risks, including the risk that choosing one could eliminate the possibility of the others. He and Grace had about two months left to make up their minds.

Come January, they rejected all three options and chose a fourth. It offered no stability, little or no pay, and no prestige or political power. But it aligned with the desire of their hearts and what they believed to be God's desire for their lives. It gave them the opportunity to love and teach truth to a group of hippies and street kids. For twenty-five years he invested his life in theirs and received tremendous investments in his own. The process has unearthed many of the principles you've read in this book, and much more.

Worthwhile Choices

Was it worth it? Bill and Grace think so, and so do many whom they have influenced. Broken men and women have entered into successful careers, some winning honors for their valued contributions. Marriages have been restored, even after years of divorce. Bill has watched alcoholics and drug addicts come clean and victims of child abuse become capable of loving others. People in pain became successful business owners, teachers, medical professionals, pastors, and participants in other vocations too numerous to mention. But all shared a common bond. Each found hope, healing, acceptance, and love in a community that honored them for who they really were and affirmed their unique calling and contribution to our culture.

All of this occurred, not because of Bill's superior talents or the capacities of his team, but because Bill and others modeled and nurtured an environment of grace, where fallible leaders could be trusted, and fallible people could learn to trust. Where truth could be faced by people without their putting on a face. Where love did not depend on being lovable. This environment sprang, in part, from Bill's decision to trust God with his own innermost being on that hot August night.

As Bill allowed God and others to see and touch the issues of his heart, he developed genuine humility—the kind nobody likes to brag about. In humility, he gained the grace to choose vulnerability, allowing God and trusted friends to speak truth to him—even to the deepest, darkest parts of his life. Bill also gained the grace he needed to align with truth, submitting to the love of others. As he did, instead of viewing himself as the neglected, abandoned son of alcoholic parents, a new Bill began to emerge from the wreckage.

The old Bill rejected love because of his own flawed perceptions of himself. But the newly emerging Bill could receive love and give love. The old Bill couldn't let truth penetrate his heart and could only teach the *words* of truth to others. The new Bill could receive truth and transfer truth into the lives of others.

A radical transformation took place. Bill's motives began to change and, in turn, so did his values and actions. Whereas the old Bill could *do* a lot, the new Bill could really *be* somebody he and others respected, because his influence and life now flowed from his changed heart.

Bill's heart had been transformed by God in the context of a community and an environment of grace. Only God can change motives. Only God can repair broken lives. God does this through the process we have called climbing the character ladder.

When we come to the end of our capacity pursuits, we must still contend with ourselves. We come into this world with selfish motives. Our motives must change in order to become the kind of person others want to follow. Nobody wants to follow a selfish person. The problem is, just wanting to be an unselfish leader does not make a leader unselfish. Wanting to be a servant leader does not make a leader a servant. To be an unselfish servant, we must become something we cannot be by nature. Our very hearts must be changed.

This means we must come (or be brought) to the end of our self-sufficiency, or like Bill, our self-devaluation. When we do, we can accept our need of grace. At the end of self-sufficiency, we can find God-sufficiency. At the end of our lonely road of isolation, we can find and take the path to community. Coming to the end of self brings us to reliance upon God, where we gain the motivation we need to climb the character ladder.

Bill could never have made the choice he did without first coming to grips with the reality that he could not change himself. Perhaps what gripped him most was the haunting fear that he might not change, finishing the second half of his life no better than the first.

In the next two years after his decision to trust God with who he was, Bill faced numerous struggles during which God proved worthy of his trust. And none too soon! By the time the three career options came about, Bill had been on the character ladder long enough to give him the inner strength and confidence he needed to do the right thing for the right reasons. He had no idea how his decision would turn out, except for the assurance that his character would be further tested, matured, and refined by choosing to align with the truth about who he and others believed he could be.

In looking back, Bill and others can see something beyond the seemingly illogical challenges and joys of the last twenty-five years. They see a work of art in the hands of a Master, crafting spatters and splotches, dark colors and vibrant colors, into a painting that only God could pull together. Bill can look back on his life now and say, "Yes, God did that," because he knows beyond a doubt that he couldn't have done it himself. In other cases though, it can be harder to see behind the veil.

The Right Leader at the Right Time

Bruce once faced this challenge of trying to see behind the veil. Back in 1983, a board representing an organization with international influence made the decision to invite Bruce to lead their multigeneration constituency. At thirty-two years of age, Bruce felt too young for the role, and he also felt very satisfied in his current situation. He had no desire for a career change and didn't want to leave his extended family and friends, or the beautiful state of Oregon where he had grown up. So he forwarded several names of "more qualified and mature" leaders to the board. Yet, more than a year later, the board returned with the same inquiry.

This circumstance tested Bruce's values. He wanted to serve others and take responsibility for the talents God had given him, but at what cost? After several months of seeking counsel from his wife, parents, pastors, and trusted friends, Bruce concluded that his background, temperament, and training had prepared him to serve and benefit this constituency. He would relinquish the security of the known, to accept this challenging invitation into the unknown.

Ten years later, through the hard work of many people, the organization's influence had grown significantly. Both demand and results exceeded expectations. The organizational team was strong; and the financial infrastructure, built on the investments of individuals, property acquisitions, and foundations, had never been healthier. Bruce found fulfillment in the expanding opportunities to serve people in a wide variety of cultures and classes.

However, his spirit of innovation and forward-looking program choices cost him something. Progress came at a price. His leadership brought out those who did not appreciate such nontraditional ways. Those who criticized the organization soon made Bruce a central issue. Eventually, he faced a difficult decision. After he took a long look at the organization's partnerships and strategies, it became clear to Bruce that several related organizations could realign and move forward more effectively only under one condition: he must choose to resign as president.

A classic fourth-rung struggle ensued. The role Bruce had viewed so indifferently ten years earlier had now become a huge part of his life, part of his identity, part of his fulfillment. He loved his work. He really didn't want to let go. Bruce reasoned, "Why not stay? The board of directors unanimously supports me. The organization remains vibrant. Our clients are increasingly responsive to our service to them. And several new initiatives hold even greater promise. What might be lost if I left now?"

The decision came down to one of motive and values—down to fourth-rung costs and fifth-rung challenges. Bruce knew deep down that the greater good of several regional and national organizations and hundreds of smaller groups would be best served by his resignation. He also knew that several valued outcomes, such as reconciliation, integrity, and progress for minorities, could be compromised if he retained his position. He felt caught between holding on to a satisfying and influential position and following the core values of his life.

Bruce could have chosen to press ahead, while spending a great deal of time and energy defending himself and the organization against their critics. But he knew this would primarily serve his own cause, not the causes of the organizations involved. Staying would honor the man but hurt the individuals and organizations. Leaving would honor the organizations but hurt the man. Bruce faced a decision rooted in motive. Was he in this for himself or for others?

If Bruce had chosen to resign in his first year, few would have faulted him. It probably would have gone relatively unnoticed when he was only thirty-three and so new to the organization. Maybe the fit was wrong. Maybe he couldn't handle the responsibility. Maybe he just had a better offer. But after ten years of effective, dedicated service, with a larger constituency and the proven track record of a forty-three-year-old, things were much more complicated. People may brush off an untested leader, but when a tested leader makes fourth- and fifth-rung decisions, such as those Bruce faced, people stand up and take notice. What is he thinking? Why would he do such a thing? What are his actions saying about us? Must it come to this?

Still, Bruce set all this aside and did what he thought best for the greater good. He resigned. Like Bill, Bruce had no idea how things would turn out. But he was learning to ascend the rails and rungs of the character ladder, honing his skill at building a life. So he aligned with truth and paid the price, because while hanging around on the character ladder, he had found God's grace to be sufficient for his self-worth, his significance, and his security. And he had tested God's grace in relationships with others who now backed him in his decision.

In Bruce's case, his choice led to expanded influence. Sometimes this happens, but one should not count on it. Difficult choices like these ensure a maturing of character and the discovery of destiny, but they do not necessarily lead to expanded influence. The character ladder is not about gaining greater control or a higher position or a larger quantity of influence. Rather, it's about an ascent to a higher *quality* of influence, where we gain the integrity to find the right position at the right time.

Mastering the Tools

As we each participate in the making of the work of art called our lives, we must learn to master the tools God has given us. A painter has brushes, oils, and canvas. To develop character, we have principles, relationships, and environments. But reading about the tools, as you have in this book, cannot make you a master any more than reading about painting will make you a great painter. To become a painter, you must start painting. To develop character, you must begin climbing the character ladder. But how?

Begin with community. Community happens one relationship at a time; therefore it is never beyond your grasp. Although the pressures of producing "results" may keep you and your organization bound in an ongoing addiction to the shorter ladder, you can take the first steps. You will begin to see what you can truly accomplish when you find friendships in which you can explore inner needs and strengths alongside issues of capacity. So how do you start?

First, find allies who are willing to stand with you. Most great movements in art came about when artists with similar passions and goals came together to support one another. You can do the same. They may not be people whom you trust entirely at first, but they should be people who are willing to earn and keep your trust. They may be your peers, your leaders, or your followers. Even better, find some from all three groups.

You need ordinary people who will be willing to tell you the truth and who will also receive truth from you. You also need people who are willing to have fun with you. Relationships are hard work. That's why fun relationships last longer. You must cultivate and nourish fun in order for it to thrive; you do so not by hiring a stand-up comedian for your next staff meeting (although that's not such a bad idea) but by actively participating in each other's lives. Hang out with those who are willing to extend unconditional acceptance to you, rooted in their own experience of God's grace. With allies who are fun, unafraid to tell the truth, and willing to accept you at face value, you will be off to a great start.

Start small. Don't launch a community-building program. Too many organizations have been force-fed enough programs *du jour* to gag their people, no matter how good the intentions were. Your goal should be simple. Get to know these people as intimately as possible within the boundaries of your role. Let them know your goals, your dreams, and your struggles. Perhaps most important, let them know how you *feel* about your goals, dreams, and struggles. Let them know how you feel about them and their own passion to create something enduring and beautiful with their lives.

Take Time to Practice

You may have been trained in management *theory*—but community is management *practice*. You become a player-coach in a game where every mistake and every victory is shared alike. You train and are trained on the team you play with and coach. And, just as it would if you wanted to become a great artist, this kind of management takes practice, practice, and more practice.

You must commit time. The best environments are produced when a core group of people commit themselves to each other for life, no matter what. Such a commitment may be hard for some to swallow, but even committing for a definite period of time works wonders.

With such time commitments, people can let down their guard. Without them, vulnerability becomes very difficult. When someone commits themselves to us for life (as in a marriage), that commitment helps us gain the security and freedom we need to be who we really are. Committing time creates opportunities for vulnerability. Vulnerability builds trust. And sooner than we think, we will be able to encourage one another on the character ladder.

Hitting Snags

As you begin to experience the stuff of life together in community, you will begin to take notice of the true strengths you and others possess. You'll discover some other things too. You'll find weaknesses. You'll hit snags.

This is to be expected. Western culture, with its fast pace and obsession with productivity, leaves little room for people to work safely through the deeper issues of life. When you try to create an environment in which these deeper issues can be addressed, you may experience a variety of reactions. It's very much like introducing truth into a dysfunctional family. When an addict faces the truth and gets well, for instance, everyone related to the addict begins to realize how out of whack they had become in their efforts to adapt to the addict's behavior. Some acknowledge their codependence. Others face their own attempts at denial or escape. The only way for systemic, healthy change to occur is when all those in the system face the truth and realign with the new reality. We've seen this dynamic rather clearly in our workshops.

At one of our workshops, an executive team began to explore the character-ladder process, thinking they had little to learn. Most of them had been friends for years. But about halfway through, their senior leader revealed that his team really didn't know him at all.

He had been struggling for years with increasing isolation and guilt over his inability to perform in certain areas. But he didn't feel he had the freedom to tell them the truth.

At first his team felt shock. Then they felt regret at how their assumptions had hurt their teammate and leader. They determined to change their habits to align with truth rather than with false assumptions, committing themselves to authentic community. Within a few short months, what they learned from each other began to have an impact on their organization as they redesigned their roles around who they really were rather than according to the assumptions of years of organizational history.

Another team had a different experience. Uncomfortable from the outset, they fought the process tooth and nail. Eventually, they accepted the fact that even though they worked together every day, they simply did not know each other. They didn't trust one another and especially did not trust their senior leader. The process led them into increasing pain until months later, several of the team members resigned, convinced they could not live in an environment where their teammates and leaders neglected the rungs and rails of the character ladder.

Some people and organizations won't make the shift. Indeed, shifting organizationally is virtually impossible without the ownership of top leaders. But whether the shift comes now or comes later, it will inevitably come. Short-ladder organizations, the kind that use people rather than build them, will not survive long when faced with competition from those that foster communities of grace.

Which organization would you rather work for? Which do you think will last through the tough times? Which will enable ordinary people to do extraordinary things?

Community is the context for the development of character. It is the context for going above and beyond our individual best, for developing extraordinary character and influence. Whatever obstacles we face on the way, the benefits far outweigh the risks. And getting started is as simple as speaking to the person in the next cubicle, or office, or pew.

Thy Will Be Done

Climbing the character ladder may lead you to the business world, the educational world, or the political, scientific, or artistic worlds. God has different plans for each of us. For Bill, choosing to climb the character ladder led to a decision to lead a church instead of a CPA firm. For Bruce, the climb led to helping a large number of people through leadership of a nonprofit organization, rather than through corporate leadership. For most it will lead to the market-place. CPA firms, governments, corporations, and families need leaders too. Every area of life and every relationship needs someone who can breathe grace, truth, and love into it.

God's plan could mean stepping up to a challenge. It could mean stepping down. But each step brings us closer to our destiny if it leads to greater love for God and others. Whether our sphere of influence is small or large, the possibilities remain the same. We can watch our motives transform from selfishness to selflessness. We can submit to the Master's loving hand, becoming what we need to become for the benefit of others and our world.

Will we accept only that which we can accomplish on our own? Or will we begin to climb the longer ladder, trusting God to lead us to a destiny far greater than we can imagine? Dr. Martin Luther King Jr. said each of us "must decide whether [we] will walk in the light of creative altruism or in the darkness of destructive selfish-ness."[1] The latter comes naturally. The former comes supernaturally. We can only live for the benefit of others when we cease living solely for ourselves and live as the Creator intended: loving God and loving others.

A few years ago at the Seattle Special Olympics, nine contes-tants, all physically or mentally disabled, assembled at the starting line for the hundred-yard dash. At the gun, they all started out—not exactly in a dash, but with a relish to run the race to the finish and win. All, that is, except one little boy, who stumbled on the as-phalt, tumbled over a couple of times, and began to cry. The other eight heard the boy cry. They slowed down, paused, and looked back. Then they all turned around and went back. Every one of them. One girl with Down's Syndrome bent over, kissed him, and said, "This will make it better." Then all nine linked arms and walked together to the finish line. Everyone in the stadium stood, and the cheering went on for several minutes.[2]

This story, recounted by an unknown author, has been told and retold by countless people. Why? Because hearing about ordinary people doing extraordinary things strikes a chord in our souls. Most likely, this story will be passed on to the next generation, because deep down in our hearts we know that helping others win matters far more than winning a hollow victory for ourselves. But like those disabled children, changing our course requires us to pause and hear the cries of those around us. Changing our course also requires us to pause and hear the cry within our own hearts.

What we do matters less than who we are. How we do things matters less than for whom we do them. As we look back at the work of art called a life, who we became and whom we served will expose our true intent. Who we became and whom we served will expose whether we climbed both ladders or relied solely on our capacities. The rails and rungs we choose will determine the destiny we receive and the legacy we will leave.

But we must take the first step. C. S. Lewis wrote, "There are only two kinds of people in the end; those who say to God, 'Thy will be done,' and those to whom God says, in the end, 'Thy will be done.'"[3] We know what leaders look like when they choose to do things their way, alone on the capacity ladder. We think our culture is ready for leaders who climb a different ladder. Do you? We think we're ready for relationships of vulnerability and trust, for leaders who align with truth and pay the price of living lives of integrity. We think we're ready for authentic environments of grace to sprout up all over the world. Do you?

A woman once had a dream in which she wandered into a shop at the mall and found Jesus behind a counter. "You can have anything your heart desires," Jesus said to her. Astounded but pleased, she asked for peace, love, happiness, wisdom, and freedom from fear. Then she added, "Not just for me, but for the whole earth."

Jesus smiled and said, "I think you misunderstand me. We don't sell fruits, only seeds."[4]

For the sake of our children and their children, we need to take the first step now. The seed of destiny within each of us awaits the day when it will bear fruit in the lives of others. It awaits the fertile soil of community. It awaits an environment of grace.

Every work of art begins with small but significant choices. Each masterpiece reveals how well the artist knew her tools, her own intentions, and her own heart. In the making of our own lives, some choices must inevitably be left to the Master. But God leaves many of the choices to us. We participate in the creation of this work of art called our life.

The ascent of a leader begins with the choices we make about which walls to climb and how to use the ladders. We need to look no further than the ordinary relationships around us to start developing the extraordinary character and influence for which we strive. And the time to begin our ascent is now.

Grabbing Hold

- Whom do you trust with you? Whom are you willing to trust with you?
- What benefits of selflessness and interdependence can you list? How can you become selfless and interdependent?
- Who are your allies in your climb up the character ladder? Where can you find more allies?
- Where will you begin to build a community of grace? How will it be sustained?

Notes

Preface

1. Peterson, 1993, p. 53 and p. 112. Also see Matthew 18:4 and Mark 10:15.

Introduction

1. Newport and Saad, 1997; Briggs, 1994.
2. Toney and Oster, 1997.
3. Newport and Saad, 1997.

Chapter One

1. Behe, 1912. The words of Smith and the crew were recounted from survivors of the wreck and probably represent a synthesis of several accounts. The website listed in the References provides excellent analysis and eyewitness reports from the *Titanic* and many different views of Captain Smith's final moments. But as the official board of inquiry decided, Captain Smith ultimately was responsible for the catastrophe. Whether others prodded him to make such decisions has no bearing on his responsibility to evaluate his options and act with good judgment.
2. Ibid., 1912.
3. Hersey and Blanchard, 1992, p. 5.

Chapter Two

1. Clinton, 1992, p. 7.
2. Clinton, 1988.

3. See Farrar, 1995, pp. 1–41.

4. Clinton, 1988, p. 167.

5. Kouzes and Posner, 1987.

6. Barsad, cited in Jackson, 1997, p. E1.

7. See Genesis 1–3, especially Genesis 1:28.

8. For an excellent, in-depth analysis and discussion of how this poem and other ancient poems can speak to modern issues, please see Whyte, 1994.

9. Covey, 1989, p. 22.

10. Kouzes and Posner, 1987, p. 27.

11. See Luke 9:46–48.

Chapter Three

1. Schein, 1985, p. 5.

2. Ibid., p. 47.

3. Colson and Eckerd, 1991, p. 137.

4. Pollard, 1996, p. 119.

5. May, 1988, p. 173.

6. Argyris, 1962, p. 43.

7. Rookmaaker, 1978, p. 48.

8. Kouzes and Posner, 1999, p. 75.

9. Ibid., p. 76.

10. McEachern, 1998.

Chapter Four

1. Hersey and Blanchard, 1992, p. 57.

2. Ibid, p. 58.

3. See Revelation 3:14, 17; Proverbs 3:5–6; John 15:1–17; and 1 Corinthians 12:20–21 and 16:14.

4. Lewis, 1946, pp. 18–19.

5. Buford, 1994, p. 167.

6. See Romans 12:4–8 and 1 Corinthians 12:20–21.

7. Schaef and Fassel, 1988, p. 195.

8. Quoted in Hawken, 1987, p. 158.
9. "No Room at the Top?" 1999.
10. Willingham, 1997, p. 76.
11. Greenleaf, 1977, p. 257.
12. Senge and others, 1994, p. 213.
13. Kouzes and Posner, 1999, pp. 119–120.

Chapter Five

1. Stephanopoulos, 1998, pp. 44–45.
2. Friess, 1998.
3. See John 12:24.
4. See Kurtz and Ketcham, 1992, pp. 186–187. Variations on this story also may be found in other works according to other religious traditions, such as De Mello, 1988, p. 116.
5. 1 Peter 5:6.
6. Shaw, 1997, p. xii.
7. See 1 Corinthians 1:27.
8. Hesselbein, Goldsmith, Beckhard, and Schubert, 1998, p. 14.
9. See, for example, Romans 8.
10. Rudner, 1992.
11. See Genesis 20.
12. Quoted in Ziglar, 1997, p. 80.

Chapter Six

1. Rubin, 1998, p. 62.
2. Schultz and Yang, 1999, p. 152.
3. See Acts 18:24–28.

Chapter Seven

1. Bonger, 1998. The information on Vincent van Gogh's life came primarily from his own letters to his brother Theo and the memoirs of his sister-in-law, Jo van Gogh Bonger. Both can be

found on the website dedicated to Vincent's life and work: http://van-gogh.org.

2. See Luke 10:25–29.

3. See Matthew 22:40.

4. De Pree, 1989, p. 27.

5. Pollard, 1996, p. 109.

6. Zimmerman, 1981, p. 120.

7. Brilliant, 1991.

Chapter Eight

1. Quoted in Rawson, 1997.

2. Taff, Taff, and Hollihan, 1987.

3. Ibid.

4. Peterson, 1993, p. 489.

5. Ibid.

6. Ibid.

7. See Luke 19:5–9.

8. See Mark 10:17–22.

9. See, for example, Proverbs 3:34 and 1 Peter 5:6.

10. See, for example, 1 Corinthians 3:9–16 and 1 Peter 1:3–7.

Chapter Nine

1. Leifer, 1997.

2. Nash and Zullo, 1988, p. 176–177.

3. Saad, 1998.

4. Ibid.

Chapter Ten

1. Thoreau, 1854.

2. Jaworski, 1996; Hagberg, 1994; Clinton, 1995; Buford, 1994.

3. This biographical information was compiled from two sources: Gonzalez-Balado and Playfoot, 1985, and Chawla, 1992.

4. This biographical information was compiled from two sources: Mosley, 1982, and Cray, 1990.
5. Psalm 75:6–7.
6. Luke 18:14.
7. 1 Peter 5:6.
8. Peck, 1993, p. 268.
9. See Matthew 6:9–10.

Chapter Eleven

1. Hagberg, 1994, p. 174.
2. De Pree, 1997, p. 138.
3. Kurtz and Ketcham, 1992, pp. 150–151. Originally from Sadeh, 1989, p. 179.
4. Clinton, 1995, p. 369.
5. Steindl-Rast and Lebell, 1995.

Chapter Twelve

1. Adapted from a plaque hanging in the Martin Luther King Jr., National Historic Site in Atlanta.
2. Author unknown. One variation of this story can be found in Canfield and Hansen, 1993. Another can be found in Berke, 1998.
3. Lewis, 1946, p. 74.
4. Adapted from De Mello, 1988, p. 103.

References

All Bible references, except as noted, are taken from *The Holy Bible, New International Version*. Grand Rapids, Mich.: Zondervan, 1973 and 1978.

Argyris, C. *Interpersonal Competence and Organizational Effectiveness*. Homewood, Ill.: Dorsey Press and Irwin, 1962.

Behe, G. *Titanic Tidbits*. London: (n.p.). [http://www.fortunecity.com/millenium/tulip/129/tree2.html]. Oct. 1998. (Originally published 1912.)

Berke, D. "The Spiritual Vision of Interfaith Fellowship: Basic Tenets." *On Course*. [http://www.interfaithfellowship.org/oncourse/articles/berke/berke6.html]. May–June 1998.

Bonger, J. "Selections from the Memoirs of Jo van Gogh Bonger." [http://van-gogh.org/docs/memoirs/memoirs]. Oct. 1998.

Briggs, D. "Protestants Still Fill Elite Ranks." *Arizona Republic*, Dec. 16, 1994, p. A22.

Brilliant, A. *I Have Abandoned My Search for Truth, and Am Now Looking for a Good Fantasy*. Santa Barbara, Calif.: Woodbridge Press, 1991.

Buford, B. *Half Time: Changing Your Game Plan from Success to Significance*. Grand Rapids, Mich.: Zondervan, 1994.

Canfield, J., and Hansen, M. V. *Chicken Soup for the Soul: 101 Stories to Open the Heart and Rekindle the Spirit*. Deerfield Beach, Fla.: Health Communications, 1993.

Chawla, N. *Mother Teresa: The Authorized Biography*. Rockport, Mass.: Element, 1992.

Clinton, J. R. *The Making of a Leader*. Colorado Springs, Colo.: NavPress, 1988.

Clinton, J. R. *Leadership in the Nineties: Six Factors to Consider*. Altadena, Calif.: Barnabas, 1992.

Clinton, J. R. *Focused Lives: Inspirational Life-Changing Lessons from Eight Effective Christian Leaders Who Finished Well*. Altadena, Calif.: Barnabas, 1995.

Colson, C., and Eckerd, J. *Why America Doesn't Work*. Dallas, Tex.: Word, 1991.

Covey, S. *The Seven Habits of Highly Effective People*. New York: Simon & Schuster, 1989.

Cray, E. *General of the Army: George C. Marshall, Soldier and Statesman*. New York: Norton, 1990.

De Crescenzo, L. *Thus Spake Bellavista*. (A. Bardoni, trans.). New York: Grove Press, 1989.

De Mello, A. *Song of the Bird*. New York: Image Books, 1984.

De Mello, A. *Taking Flight: A Book of Story Meditations*. New York: Doubleday, 1988.

De Pree, M. *Leadership Is an Art*. New York: Dell, 1989.

De Pree, M. *Leading Without Power: Finding Hope in Serving Community*. San Francisco: Jossey-Bass, 1997.

Farrar, S. *Finishing Strong: Finding the Power to Go the Distance*. Sisters, Oreg.: Multnomah, 1995.

Friess, F. Speech presented at community leadership breakfast, Pinnacle Forum, Scottsdale, Ariz., Apr. 10, 1998.

Gonzalez-Balado, J. L., and Playfoot, J. N. (eds.). *My Life for the Poor: Mother Teresa of Calcutta*. San Francisco: Harper San Francisco, 1985.

Greenleaf, R. K. *Servant Leadership: A Journey into the Nature of Legitimate Power and Greatness*. Mahwah, N.J.: Paulist Press, 1977.

Hagberg, J. O. *Real Power: Stages of Personal Power in Organizations*. Salem, Wis.: Sheffield Publishing Company, 1994.

Harter, J. (ed.). *Thoughts on Success: Thoughts and Reflections from History's Great Thinkers*. Mineola, N.Y.: Dover, Forbes Subscriber Edition, 1995.

Hawken, P. *Growing a Business*. New York: Simon & Schuster, 1987.

Hersey, P., and Blanchard, K. H. *Management of Organizational Behavior: Utilizing Human Resources*. (2nd ed.) Upper Saddle River, N.J.: Prentice Hall, 1992.

Hesselbein, F., Goldsmith, M., Beckhard, R. and Schubert, R. (eds.). *The Community of the Future*. San Francisco: Jossey-Bass, 1998.

Jackson, M. "Bosses Held in Low Esteem and Sinking Fast, Study Says: Anger, Skepticism Fill Workplace, Survey Finds." *Arizona Republic*, Sept. 2, 1997, p. E1.

James, W. *Principles of Psychology*. New York: Dover Publications, Inc., 1979.

Jaworski, J. *Synchronicity: The Inner Path of Leadership*. San Francisco: Berrett-Koehler, 1996.

Kierkegaard, S. *Journal 1848*. (H. V. Hong and E. H. Hong, eds.). Bloomington: Indiana University Press, 1848.

Kouzes, J. M., and Posner, B. Z. *The Leadership Challenge: How to Get Extraordinary Things Done in Organizations*. San Francisco: Jossey-Bass, 1987.

Kouzes, J. M., and Posner, B. Z. *Encouraging the Heart: A Leader's Guide to Rewarding and Recognizing Others*. San Francisco: Jossey-Bass, 1999.

Kuhn, M. *Get Out There and Do Something About Injustice*. New York: Friendship Press, 1972.

Kurtz, E., and Ketcham, K. *The Spirituality of Imperfection: Storytelling and the Journey to Wholeness*. New York: Bantam Books, 1992.

Leifer, S. "Entrepreneurs' Forum in Hale Boasts a Stellar Lineup." [http://www.bus.umich.edu/news/hale.html]. Oct. 6, 1997.

Lewis, C. S. *The Great Divorce*. New York: HarperCollins, 1946.

May, G. G. *Addiction and Grace: Love and Spirituality in the Healing of Addictions*. New York: HarperCollins, 1988.

McEachern, R. Speech presented at Apple Computer, Cupertino, Calif., Dec. 1998.

Mosley, L. *Marshall: Hero for Our Times*. New York: Hearst, 1982.

Nash, B. M., and Zullo, A. *The Misfortune 500: Featuring the Business Hall of Shame*. New York: Pocket Books, 1988.

Newport, F., and Saad, L. "Religious Faith Is Widespread but Many Skip Church." Gallup Poll Archives, 1997. [http://198.175.140.8/POLL_ARCHIVES/1997/970329.htm] Oct. 1998.

"No Room at the Top? How a Big Five Accounting Firm Changed Its Culture to Support Women." CNNfn [http://cnnfn.com/fortune/9903/04/fortune_deloitte/], Mar. 4, 1999.

Norris, K. *Hands Full of Living*. Mattituck, N.Y.: Amereon, 1988.

Peck, M. S. *A World Waiting to Be Born: Civility Rediscovered*. New York: Bantam Books, 1993.

Peterson, E. H. *The Message: The New Testament in Contemporary Language*. Colorado Springs, Colo.: NavPress, 1993.

Pollard, C. W. *The Soul of the Firm*. Grand Rapids, Mich.: Zondervan, 1996.

Prolificus. "Quotes about Wisdom." [http://www.prolificus.com/commongenius/wisdom.html], May 11, 1999.

Rawson, H. *Unwritten Laws: The Unofficial Rules of Life*. New York: Crown, 1997.

Redmoon, A. "Quotes About Fear." [http://www.quoteland.com/quotes/author/388.html]. Apr. 22, 1999.

Rookmaaker, H. R. *Art Needs No Justification*. Downers Grove, Ill.: InterVarsity Press, 1978.

Rubin, H. "Peter's Principles." *Inc.*, Mar. 1, 1998.

Rudner, R. *Naked Beneath My Clothes: Tales of a Revealing Nature*. New York: Penguin, 1992.

Saad, L. " 'Most Admired' Poll Finds Americans Lack Major Heroes: Mother Teresa's Death Leaves a Void on List of Most Admired Women." Gallup Poll Archives, 1998. [http://198.175.140.8/POLL_ARCHIVES/980101.htm].

Sadeh, P. *Jewish Folktales*. (H. Halkin, trans.). New York: Doubleday, 1989.

Saint Exupéry, A. de. *The Wisdom of the Sands* (S. Gilbert, trans.). Orlando: Harcourt Brace, 1950.

Schaef, A. W., and Fassel, D. *The Addictive Organization: Why We Overwork, Cover Up, Pick Up the Pieces, Please the Boss and Perpetuate Sick Organizations*. San Francisco: Harper San Francisco, 1988.

Schein, E. H. *Organizational Culture and Leadership*. San Francisco: Jossey-Bass, 1985.

Schultz, H., and Yang, D. J. *Pour Your Heart Into It: How Starbucks Built a Company One Cup at a Time*. New York: Hyperion, 1999.

Senge, P., and others. *The Fifth Discipline Fieldbook*. New York: Doubleday, 1994.

Shaw, R. B. *Trust in the Balance: Building Successful Organizations on Results, Integrity, and Concern*. San Francisco: Jossey-Bass, 1997.

Steindl-Rast, D., and Lebell, S. *The Music of Silence: Entering the Sacred Space of Monastic Experience*. (Sound recording). Los Angeles: Audio Renaissance Tapes, 1995.

Stephanopoulos, G. *All Too Human: A Political Education*. Boston: Little, Brown. 1999

Taff, R., Taff, T., and Hollihan, J. "Healing Touch." In *Russ Taff*. Sound recording. Waco, Tex.: Word Records, 1987.

Thoreau, H. D. *Walden*. [http://www2.cybernex.net/~rlenat/walden00.html]. (Originally published 1854.)

Toney, F., and Oster, M. *The Leader and Religious Faith: The Relationship Between the Exercise of Religious Faith by CEOs and Goal Achievement, Self-Fulfillment, and Social Benefits*. Self-published study, 1997.

Whyte, D. *The Heart Aroused: Poetry and the Preservation of the Soul in Corporate America*. New York: Doubleday, 1994.

Willingham, R. *The People Principle: A Revolutionary Redefinition of Leadership*. New York: St. Martin's Press, 1997.

Yancy, P. *Church: Why Bother? My Personal Pilgrimage*. Grand Rapids: Zondervan, 1998.

Ziglar, Z. *Over the Top*. Nashville, Tenn.: Thomas Nelson, 1997.

Zimmerman, M. E. *Eclipse of the Self*. Athens: Ohio University Press, 1981.

The Authors

Bill Thrall serves as leadership mentor for Leadership Catalyst, a nonprofit organization dedicated to cultural change through the training of leaders in character, relationships, and influence. Prior to joining Leadership Catalyst, he led Open Door Fellowship in Phoenix, a church he founded in 1973. He has pastored others for three decades, providing rich benefits to many leaders. Before his involvement in vocational ministry, he was a CPA and management consultant. He and his wife, Grace, have three married children—Bill, Wende, and Joy—and seven grandchildren.

Bruce McNicol guides Leadership Catalyst as president, applying his extensive international work experience and degrees in finance law, theology, and leadership development. He stands alongside leaders, providing mentoring, networks, and resources to help them reach their full potential. From 1985 to 1995, he served as president of Interest Associates, based in Chicago. In that role, he brokered organizational partnerships, secured funding for urban groups, and helped leaders from eleven cultures establish more than one hundred churches in North America. He is married to Janet, who is a homemaker and nurse. They have three children, Nicole, Chad, and Ryan.

Ken McElrath has a dual passion. An artist at heart, he is always creating. Whether crafting organizational change, remodeling his home, or dabbling with an oil painting, he thrives on challenging the status quo. He also aspires to see creativity permeate the lives of leaders and the cultures they construct. After holding marketing and design positions with various organizations, he earned his way to becoming director of marketing with a Fortune 500 company and then helped launch Leadership Catalyst, serving as director of marketing and product development. His wife, Donna, works with disadvantaged urban youth in Phoenix. They have three children, Zach, Tommy, and Anne.

About Leadership Network

The mission of Leadership Network is to accelerate the emergence of effective churches by identifying and connecting innovative church leaders and providing them with resources in the form of new ideas, people, and tools. Churches and church leaders served by Leadership Network represent a wide variety of primarily Protestant faith traditions that range from mainline to evangelical to independent. All are characterized by innovation, entrepreneurial leadership and a desire to be on the leading edge of ministry.

Leadership Network's focus has been on the practice and application of faith at the local congregational level. A partner with Leadership Network, the Leadership Training Network uses peer learning and interactive training to accelerate the equipping church movement through gift-based team ministry.

Established as a private foundation in 1984 by social entrepreneur Bob Buford, Leadership Network is acknowledged as an influential leader among churches and faith-based ministries and a major resource to which innovative church leaders turn for networking and information.

For additional information on Leadership Network, please contact:

Leadership Network
2501 Cedar Springs, Suite 200
Dallas, Texas 75201
800-765-5323
www.leadnet.org

Index